KV-513-986

THE OPEN UNIVERSITY
DEPARTMENT OF HEALTH AND SOCIAL WELFARE
IN ASSOCIATION WITH
THE HEALTH EDUCATION AUTHORITY

DRUG USE

& MISUSE

THE OPEN UNIVERSITY PRESS

Course Team

Open University

Vic Finkelstein *Course Team Chair/Senior Lecturer*
Marjorie Gott *Lecturer*
Janet Grant *Senior lecturer*
Tom Heller *Senior lecturer*
Carole Jeffery *Course co-ordinator*
Caroline Malone *Course co-ordinator*
David Inglis *Editor*
Rob Williams *Designer*
Keith Howard *Graphic artist*
Paul Smith *Liaison librarian*
Antonet Roberts *Secretarial support*
Ouida Rice *Developmental testing*
Janice Dale *Developmental testing*
Malcolm Johnson *Reading member*

BBC Open University Production Centre

Ann Pointon *Producer*
Jan Read *Production assistant*

External assessor

Martin A. Plant, BSc, MA, PhD *Senior Research Fellow, Alcohol Research Group, Department of Psychiatry, University of Edinburgh*

Authors

Nicholas Dorn *Assistant Director (Research), Institute for the Study of Drug Dependence*
Geoffrey Pearson *Professor of Social Work, Faculty of Social Science, Middlesex Polytechnic*
Bruce Ritson *Consultant Psychiatrist and Senior Lecturer, Department of Psychiatry, University of Edinburgh, Royal Edinburgh Hospital*
Nigel South *Research Officer, Institute for the Study of Drug Dependence*
David Turner *Co-ordinator, Standing Conference on Drug Abuse*
Rowdy Yates *Director, The Lifeline Project, Manchester*
Phil Evans *Cartoonist*

Acknowledgements

The course team gratefully acknowledge the contribution of the following consultants
Dr. Brendan Bradley *Department of Psychology, Institute of Psychiatry, University of London*
Dr. Michael Gossop *Drug Dependence Unit, Bethlem Royal Hospital*
Dr. Larry Ray *Department of Sociology, University of Lancaster*
David McNally *Lifeline Project*

The course team wish to thank the many participants in the developmental testing of the course materials and the organizations who provided information and assistance in the production of these materials, especially the Institute for the Study of Drug Dependence Library and Information Service, the Lifeline Project, and the North West Regional Drug Training Unit.

This study pack is the second in the series 'Education for Health' funded by the Health Education Authority.

The Open University, Walton Hall, Milton Keynes MK7 6AA
First published 1987
Copyright © 1987 The Open University
All rights reserved. No part of this publication may be reproduced, stored in a retrieval system or transmitted, in any form or by any means, without written permission from the publisher.
Designed by the Graphic Design Group of the Open University.
Printed in Great Britain by Foister & Jagg Ltd., Abbey Walk, Cambridge.
ISBN 0 335 11315 X
Further information on Open University Continuing Education courses may be obtained from the Associate Student Central Office, The Open University, PO Box 76, Walton Hall, Milton Keynes MK7 6AN.

CONTENTS

Please note:
Some activity numbers have been changed on the audio cassette.
These changes have been noted in the activity boxes.

WELCOME TO THE COURSE

The preparation of this course on drug use and misuse has been a challenging exercise, perhaps not surprisingly as the subject area involves many vested interests, moral and educational issues, political and law and order considerations as well as welfare, health and medical concerns. We, on the course team, have, however, enjoyed the opportunity of learning more about this difficult subject area and, in welcoming you to your studies, we wish you an equally enjoyable and rewarding experience.

These materials have been designed for individual home study and the pack includes all the material you need in order to complete the course. The course materials include this workbook, a Reader containing all the readings you will be required to study as you work through the main study text, and an audio cassette which provides additional material to highlight important issues covered in the main text. A video has also been prepared for use in group work with these learning materials.

The workbook is your main study text and it will guide you through the learning materials and from time to time ask you to carry out a number of learning 'activities'. These activities are clearly marked in red shaded areas in the text and they are designed to encourage more *active* learning during your study of the course. The learning activities may ask you to review or critically study a paper in the Reader, to listen to the audio cassette and make notes, or to carry out some other task, like gathering information about drug users in your local community. Notes made when carrying out a learning activity should always be kept (perhaps in a loose leaf folder or ring binder) so that you can refer to them as you work through other chapters in the workbook.

The study pack has been designed for use by students with a variety of backgrounds and different experiences of drug use and misuse. The course does not set out to promote a particular view of drug usage, or a favoured approach which the course team would like to see adopted by students. Nevertheless, chapter authors have, of course, presented and discussed some of their own views and preferred approaches. We hope, however, that when you have completed your studies you will agree that we have presented a balanced view and that the course has assisted you in feeling more confident about making up your own mind regarding the kind of approach that best seems to suit you. With this in mind we have tried to encourage you to examine your own attitudes and practices. It is important to sound a warning here, however, for no correspondence text can teach all aspects of practice skills. Do bear in mind, therefore, as you work through the text, that although you will be introduced to different practical approaches, and the skills that go with them, there is a limit to how much these learning materials can help you to acquire these skills.

The course work has been divided into seven chapters:

1 Introduction
In this chapter we ask you to look at your own attitudes towards drugs and their use and we try to set the scene for your study of the workbook by introducing some of the central, sometimes controversial, issues raised by drug use.

2 Drugs and their effects
This chapter looks at the nature of drugs, examines their effects on users and discusses the situations in which people are likely to take drugs. The influence of the users' expectations and the setting in which drugs are used are also examined.

3 Drug use and misuse
In this chapter drug use is examined in its social context. We discuss the importance of looking at the way people make their decisions when moving from experiment to dependency, or stopping use. And the influence of local attitudes and conditions in providing the context for drug use is stressed.

4   The control of drugs

This chapter looks at the various ways societies have tried to control the distribution of some drugs while tolerating, or even encouraging, the marketing of others.

5   Intervention approaches

Different approaches to intervention are examined and we discuss possible reasons behind the introduction of these approaches, their development, or withdrawal.

6   Treatment skills

In this chapter we present some of the practical approaches that have been introduced for work with drug users. Skills which have been found useful in working with drug users are also identified.

7   Summary and looking forward

The final chapter highlights the main themes, issues and approaches raised in the pack.

The preparatory activity, below, is designed to provide material which you may refer to in study activities in later chapters in the course.

ACTIVITY
NEWSPAPER CUTTINGS

You are expected to spend 5 minutes each day for a week on this activity.

You are asked to collect your daily newspapers for one week. Go through each paper and mark all the references that mention, in any way, drugs or drug usage. Try underlining the opinions in a different coloured ink from the facts. Accumulated old newspapers will do just as well for this activity.

Comment

At the time of the preparation of this course there was an increase in measures undertaken by the USA and great concern was expressed in the daily papers about the possible spread of the 'drugs epidemic' to this country. Very strong views were being expressed about increased heroin use and the danger of new forms of cocaine entering the UK market.

1.1 ATTITUDES AND DRUGS

We all use drugs at some time. Drugs used include alcohol, nicotine, caffeine in tea and coffee, pain killers or prescription pills from a doctor. Use may be occasional, like having a cigarette only after meals, or frequent, like drinking a large number of cups of tea during the day. Drugs, of course, are used for a variety of reasons: as part of social intercourse, as a relaxant after work, or as a stimulant to keep us going under trying conditions. How different, we may ask, is this behaviour from that of the behaviour of those labelled as drug misusers? Should the number of injuries and deaths associated with smoking and drinking be regarded as somehow different casualty figures from those associated with illicit drug use?

MORAL CONCERNS

Nowadays it is difficult to pick up a newspaper or popular journal, watch the television, or listen to the radio, without having our attention drawn to some form of drug use or misuse. 'Drugs ''rife in City'' ', for example, is a typical headline in a national newspaper, referring to the use of illicit drugs by some City businessmen at their place of work. From time to time, however, there seems to be a noticeable increase in the frequency of these stories, in the number and range of people involved and in the strength of feeling expressed. It has been suggested that these 'moral panics', as they have been called, might be started by powerful vested interests who wish to divert attention from other problems, such as poverty, unemployment, and so on.

ACTIVITY 1.1
'MORAL PANICS'

Take about 20 minutes for this activity.

Read 'Solvent sniffing as a moral panic' by Richard Ives, in the Reader. When you have read the paper write a paragraph on whether you regard the term 'moral panic' as a useful way of describing strong reactions to drug use.

Comment

During the 1960s, there did seem to be a moral panic around the use of cannabis. The users were seen as rejecting the values of capitalism because the 'work ethic' in a wealthy society was considered quite unnecessary and socialism was seen as more repressive on personal freedom. Perhaps, however, criticism of drug user behaviour seems less like a moral panic when we look at the 1960s' optimism about abundant riches from the hindsight of the 1980s?

Heroin, alcohol, solvents and other drugs used in bad conditions lead to bad consequences; and there certainly has been an increase in the extent of drug use and an increase in related drug problems (Pearson, 1987). Some users of solvents, illegal drugs and even alcohol also seem to enjoy playing the stereotype role of 'youth gone wrong' (Ives, 1986) – sometimes with consequences that are frightening or otherwise unacceptable to those around them (such as burglaries). From this point of view public concern about drug related problems may be realistic and not simply examples of 'moral panics' imposed upon innocent young people by powerful forces.

However, there is a sense in which the term 'moral panic' may be useful. Assuming that drug use will never be completely eradicated, a good case can be made out for harm minimalization policies. The government's approach to drug use is, however, (in 1987) still ambivalent. Whilst AIDS publicity campaigns suggest that people who take drugs should not inject, and that if they really *must* inject, they do so with sterilized needles, the government's anti-heroin campaign remains silent about the possibility of reducing harmful practices. There seems to be a fear that promoting safer drug use will be seen as a moral defence of the activity.

PERSONAL ATTITUDES

Social attitudes towards drug use can contain both rational and irrational feelings. While it may not be possible for any of us to be completely rational and uninfluenced by prevailing social attitudes towards drug use, it seems reasonable at least to try to become a little more aware of any ambiguities in our own feelings towards drug use, and misuse, and the reasons why we may be concerned or involved with this subject.

ACTIVITY 1.2
DRUGS: PERSONAL LIKES
AND DISLIKES

Take 15 minutes over this activity.

In this activity you are asked to make a selected list of ten substances which you feel are good examples of drugs. Do not only list illicit drugs, such as heroin, but think of everyday substances, like coffee, as well as licit drugs, such as tobacco. When you have completed the list identify those drugs about which you have negative feelings, fear, or rejection, etc., and those drugs which you find attractive, pleasurable or acceptable. Now write a sentence or two about why you are interested in drug use and your reasons for studying *Drug Use and Misuse*.

All Classes, Ages and Sexes
DRINK
Coca-Cola
The Satisfactory Beverage
It satisfies the thirst and pleases the palate. Relieves the fatigue that comes from over-work, over-shopping or over-play. Puts vim and go into tired brains and bodies.
Cooling-Refreshing-Delicious, Thirst-Quenching
Guaranteed under the Pure Food and Drugs Act, June 30, 1906. Serial No. 3324.
5c. Everywhere

Comment

The range of substances which might be regarded as drugs is enormous. Nevertheless, there are substances, like heroin, which most people will agree are drugs, however they may react towards them. In my list I noted strong feelings of anxiety towards substances like heroin, opium, barbiturates, cocaine and tobacco (despite, or perhaps because of, being an ex-smoker). Coffee and tea are attractive, but I feel neutral towards aspirin and vitamin C. I also noted rather mixed feelings towards marijuana and alcohol. Although the consumption of drugs affects us all, our motivations for involvement or non-involvement will be different. Keep the notes made for this activity and compare your views with those presented elsewhere in the course, such as in Chapters 2 and 3.

HISTORICAL CHANGES

Drugs are taken both for their psychological and their physical effects, and they may be used for a variety of reasons, such as to cure illnesses, because they seem to help people relax and sleep, or because they stimulate our senses and make us feel alert, and so on. However, all drugs are not seen in the same way. Some have been welcomed and accepted by society while others are rejected because they are seen as dangerous or undesirable.

However, substances which are regarded as unacceptable in one society may be quite acceptable in another. Even within one culture fashions change and drugs which were considered acceptable may later be rejected as dangerous. Cocaine, for example, was available as an ingredient of Coca-Cola until early in the 1900s and morphine and laudanum, which were processed from opium, were widely used in patent medicines for a large range of ailments and conditions such as sleeplessness and all manner of aches and pains.

There are many other reasons why drugs may be cultivated and used. Ganja-smoking in Jamaica, for example, was said to have been taken up by anti-colonialists as part of their cultural development which rejected colonial values (Chapter 4 takes this discussion further). Armed rebels, too, have seen the cultivation of drug producing crops as a valuable source of cash for weapons. History shows, therefore, that cultural attitudes towards drug use are not based upon rational considerations of their harmful effects.

1.2   THE PLACE OF DRUGS IN THE ECONOMY

Concern about drug misuse in the industrial countries has led to the development of several approaches designed to restrict access to illicit drugs. Chief amongst these is the attempt to reduce drug production at its source, that is, to restrict cultivation of drug yielding crops in Third World countries. The debate for and against this policy can be quite bewildering and often depends upon whether the argument is coming from an exporter or importer country. It can be argued, for example, that the Third World producer is simply obeying well established laws of supply and demand and that it is not appropriate for First World countries to intervene in Third World economies but rather for them to improve their own measures for reducing demand. In any case, the argument continues, Third World countries are at the receiving end of massive export drives from First World manufacturers of licit drugs (including cigarettes and alcohol), some of which are just as harmful as the illicit drugs.

DRUGS AND THE WORLD ECONOMY

Whatever the merits of the different sides of the argument, one thing is clear; that drug production, distribution and marketing is big business, so big, in fact, that some national economies can become dependent upon the 'drugs economy' (Henman et al, 1985).

A typical cycle of heroin or cocaine production involves a peasant farmer who, although receiving very little, gets a great deal more ready cash than can ever be expected from legal crops. Then the base material is exported to a second country where it undergoes chemical processing and preparation for bulk transportation to a third country where it is diluted and divided into smaller quantities for final sale to the consumer. 'Value increases by a factor of anything from 125 per cent to 1000 per cent in its transition from raw material to finished product. The profit margin for the refiners is clearly substantial even after transport, labour and protection costs have been deducted' (ibid., p. 10).

Apart from providing the small scale peasant farmer with a source of income the production and marketing of illegal drugs can also be seen as an important way of bringing capital into a Third World country when all other avenues are blocked because of the country's low economic level or because the major profitable crops are already controlled by foreign creditors. The opium trade with China in the early nineteenth century, after all, was one of the ways that the British East India Company accumulated fabulous wealth.

When a Third World Country has economic difficulties, and large foreign debts, income from illegal drugs can assume ever greater significance for the whole economy. Destroying these crops in response to requests from First World countries could mean destroying the economy. Perhaps it is no wonder, then, that where illicit drug production has gained a major foothold in the economy of a country it is virtually impossible to eradicate.

A CASE IN POINT: TOBACCO

Historically, of course, like alcohol but unlike opium, economic and political factors did not lead to tobacco being made illegal but rather to its integration into national economies and international trading relations. While acknowledging the health issues associated with tobacco, for example, successive British governments have been wary of doing anything about it, as Mr Ian MacLeod, the Minister of Health in Winston Churchill's Conservative government of 1952–54 said: 'Smokers, mainly cigarette smokers, contribute some £1000 million yearly to the Exchequer and none knows better than the government that they simply cannot afford to lose so much' (Taylor, 1984, p. 5).

Taylor (ibid.), uses the term 'smoke ring' to describe the ring of political and economic interests that protects the tobacco industry. For governments their involvement in the 'smoke ring' provides not just revenue but:

● tens of thousands of jobs in hard economic times

● a healthy surplus on the balance of payments

● development in Third World tobacco producing countries.

Chapter 4 discusses these points in more detail.

1.3   SIZE OF THE PROBLEM

It is obviously difficult to gather accurate information into the vast area of legal and illegal drug use. Part of this difficulty is due to continual changes in drug availability, changes in drug using behaviour and difficulties in detecting illegal behaviours which tend to be carried out in secret. Problems in deciding what is a drug add to the confusion. Nevertheless, it is useful at this stage in your studies to get some overview of drug use in the UK.

ACTIVITY 1.3
DRUG INDICATORS PROJECT

Spend 15 minutes on this activity.

Read 'Patterns of drug taking in Britain' by Hartnoll *et al.* in the Reader. Make a note of the significant illicit drugs that are currently in use and list some of the changes that have happened recently in substance choice.

Comment

The most widely used illicit drug is cannabis. The use of cannabis by all classes has changed the meaning of cannabis use from its former status as a symbol of an 'alternative' culture. Although publicity about solvent sniffing, at the time of going to print, had declined dramatically over the past few years, Hartnoll *et al.* suggests that there has been an increase in this form of drug taking. Note how many of the drugs covered in this activity were also listed by you in Activity 1.2.

STEREOTYPES

The major stereotype is probably concerned with the idea of a 'drug pusher' waiting to 'lure' young people into drug dependency (Plant, 1987, p. 2). The evidence discussed in Chapter 3 is that experimentation with drugs is most frequently undertaken in the company of friends. Similarly, popular stereotypes about drug users as dirty, long-haired and derelicts are equally groundless. In Activity 1.2 you were asked to look at your personal substance likes and dislikes and it is interesting to see how we may use one drug, such as

alcohol or tobacco, without recognizing it as such, while maintaining an abhorrence of dangerous drugs, such as heroin.

WOMEN AND DRUGS

The differences between male and female drug use appear to be slowly changing. There are increasing numbers of women using psychotropic drugs, alcohol and tobacco (ibid., p. 93). However, the context in which women use, or stop using, drugs is different to men (see 'Women and drug use' by Edith Gomberg in the Reader for more discussion on this) and when these contexts are ignored meaningful intervention is unlikely, even when, as with smoking during pregnancy, the potentially harmful effects are known to the smokers.

ACTIVITY 1.4
'SMOKING IN PREGNANCY'

Spend 20 minutes on this activity.

There has been widespread publicity on smoking during pregnancy and few mothers can be unaware of its ill-effects on the unborn child. In 'Smoking in pregnancy' Hilary Graham approached this problem by interviewing mothers on their attitudes towards smoking during pregnancy. You should now read this paper in the Reader and make brief notes of the main points.

Comment

Graham suggests that health education in this area might have been inappropriate because it focusses largely on warning mothers of the harm which smoking might cause the foetus. What it fails to do, however, is to take account of the context in which women smoke. For example, by suggesting that women who smoke are being irresponsible to the foetus, health education forgets that pregnant mothers will often have many responsibilities, to their other children, to their husbands and to wider family networks. Smoking a cigarette might be a means by which some women carve out a little time for themselves during a busy day, thus enabling them to avoid continuous and excessive pressure and to carry out their responsibilities to other family members more adequately.

ACTIVITY 1.5
A WOMAN'S POINT OF VIEW

Spend 30 minutes on this activity.

Listen to the audio cassette on Carol talking about how she started taking drugs and how she feels women drug users are seen. You will be asked to make some notes while listening.

After listening note differences in the situation in which you think men and women might use licit or illicit drugs.

Comment

Thinking of alcohol consumption Chapter 3 examines the context in which people start and continue to use drugs, and notes that although the situation is changing, men are much more likely to drink in the company of men friends in pubs whereas women drink more frequently in their homes or those of relatives and friends. Keep your notes made during this Activity for reference in Chapters 3 and 6.

RACE AND DRUGS

While research looking at the use of drugs by women is limited, but growing, there is still a major gap in any information about the use of drugs by different ethnic groups. Perhaps there is some significance in this, since people with different ethnic backgrounds are prone to stereotyping as drug users and stereotyping thrives on ignorance.

THE PROBLEM IN YOUR OWN LOCAL AREA

It is not possible to make an accurate calculation of drug misuse in the community (Hartnoll *et al.*, 1986). At best we can make a rough estimation but this can be very helpful when working in the field and trying to decide what services are most needed.

ACTIVITY 1.6
FINDING OUT ABOUT SOURCES OF DRUG INFORMATION IN YOUR OWN COMMUNITY

Spend 20 minutes on this activity.

Make a note of all the possible sources of statistics and information that might assist you in building up a picture of drug use in your community.

Comment

Sources of information will vary in different localities. National statistical surveys can provide a framework for identifying ways of classifying local information. Your local library may be a good source of information about statistics in your area and the nearest health authority for guidance on death rates and incidence of drug use. Police statistics could be useful sources of information, especially when linked with Home Office statistics and Court Reports. Sometimes the librarian in the local university or polytechnic may be able to direct you to local community research projects and reports. Community specialist agencies, local doctors specializing in treatment, or teachers in the local school with responsibility for education about drug use, may also be able to provide information.

ACTIVITY 1.7
BUILDING UP THE PICTURE

2 hours (This activity is optional.)

You may want to actually start to undertake a local survey using the information you can obtain from the above sources. Of course this does not have to be done all at once, but you may want to start to look for the information to build up a more complete picture in the course of the next few weeks or months.

A more effective way of gathering information is to get together with some of your local colleagues who are interested in this subject, or who may also be studying this course, and work together to build up a more complete profile. The ISDD *Surveys and Statistics on Drugtaking in Britain* is a useful guide to additional information sources for this activity.

Comment

The extent of drug use is very patchy. In some areas the indications may be that there seems to be very little problem, although all the apparently necessary social conditions are present. In some towns the patterns of drug use are very different in areas which apparently share almost identical prevailing conditions. You may like to reflect on why the pattern of drug use that you have found in your own locality has developed in the way that it has.

1.4   HOW SHOULD DRUG USE BE INTERPRETED?

The persistence of illicit drug use, despite widespread publicity campaigns and severe policing, needs to be understood in order to devise more effective preventative and therapeutic policies. One approach has been to see drug users as ill people in need of medical intervention. This model has dominated interpretations of drug use for some time and it may be informative to examine this model in more detail.

THE DISEASE MODEL OF DRUG USE

All those working with drug users agree that a relationship of trust is important to any treatment approach. However, such trust has to be built on mutual understanding between the drug user and the helper. If alcoholism, for example, is regarded as a disease then this will result in a specific approach to treatment, with its own appropriate skills. If it is regarded as inappropriate learned behaviour then this in turn will lead to a different treatment regime.

We have introduced the next paper as background reading for your study of Chapters 5 and 6 because it nicely highlights some of the implications of choosing one interpretation over another for something like alcohol misuse.

ACTIVITY 1.8 'IS ALCOHOLISM A DISEASE?'

Spend 15 minutes on this activity.

Read 'Is alcoholism a disease?' by Nick Heather and Ian Robertson, in the Reader. On completing your study of this paper draw up a check list of pros and cons on the use of a disease model of drug use. Can you think of other ways to interpret drug misuse?

Comment

In the disease model of drug misuse, it is believed that certain people are particularly vulnerable to substances, such as alcohol and certain psychotropic drugs. The belief is that if these substances are misused there will be an inevitable development of habitual use and dependency. The condition is also said to be incurable and present in that individual for the rest of their life. There are other versions of the disease model, which are discussed in greater detail in Chapter 5. These include the 'personality disorder' model which interprets the behaviour of the drug user as the consequence of a distorted or sick personality. The use of drugs is seen as an attempt by the user to resolve personal conflicts. However, this is futile as long as the personality remains disordered, and results in a vicious circle of drug use leading to further personal conflicts and the need for more drugs.

In the 'spiritual problem' model drug misuse is seen as an attempt by the user to fill a void left by the decline in spiritual and religious values in our society. The use of drugs, however, is seen as leading to personal moral decline thus setting up another vicious circle of drug misuse. The 'social problem' model interprets drug misuse as a way of trying to cope with social circumstances – unemployment, for example, is seen as a factor which may lead to drug use. The 'risk taking' model has been devised to explain some features in the development from adolescence to adulthood. This model was developed in the late 1970s when solvent sniffing increased amongst the youth. The drug consumption was not large but it was interpreted as a form of adolescent experimentation.

THE PROFESSIONAL DILEMMA

The variety of social reactions to drugs and the way they are used provides those working in the 'field' with a wide range of interpretations, and models, for explaining the prevalence of drug use in all human societies. Nevertheless, there are real dilemmas in trying to explain why certain drugs are legal, such as tobacco with its well established harmful effects, whereas other drugs which are less dangerous remain illicit. Does this mean that the worker in the field should remain silent about the licit, but dangerous, drugs while campaigning against the illicit drugs? Perhaps this dilemma is both part of the drug 'problem' and a real reflection of the ambiguous social attitudes towards drug use.

DRUGS AND THEIR EFFECTS

In this introductory chapter we have tried to provide a broad historical context for the more detailed discussions in the following chapters. We have pointed out that drug use is common to all human societies and that under special circumstances the production of drugs can assume a very significant role in maintaining the economy of certain states. We have tried to highlight some of the difficulties in making sense of the wide range of attitudes towards drugs. In the next chapter you begin a more detailed examination of drug use by looking at drugs and their effects.

REFERENCES

Gomberg, E.S.L. (1982) 'Historical and political perspective: women and drug use', *J. Soc. Issues, vol. 38, no. 2*

Henman, A., Lewis, R. & Malyon, T. (1985) *Big Deal: the politics of the illicit drugs business,* Pluto Press

Malyon, T. (1985) 'Love seeds and cash crops – the cannabis commodity market', in Henman *et al.* (1985) Pluto Press

Pearson, G. (1987) *The new heroin users: voices from the street,* Blackwell

Plant, M.A. (1987) *Drugs in perspective,* Hodder & Stoughton

Taylor, P. (1984) *Smoke ring: the politics of tobacco,* Bodley Head

2 DRUGS AND THEIR EFFECTS

2.1 INTRODUCTION

In this chapter we will help you become clearer about what is meant by the term 'drug', and discuss some of the effects that drugs have on people who take them.

It can be surprisingly difficult to be clear about what is meant by 'drug', as it often means very different things to different people, and there are many different methods of classification.

The word probably derives originally from the Dutch *Droog* meaning dry, which referred to the dried medicinal herbs imported from the East by Dutch merchants. Drugs, commonly derived from plants, have been used from earliest times to remedy sickness and change the way we feel. They were often administered by priests or healers who would give the potion along with a particular prayer or incantation.

The symbol R_x, commonly still used by doctors on prescription pads, is in fact an Egyptian reference to a prayer. As we shall discuss, the idea of having faith in a drug, or its prescriber, is still a key determinant of the effect that it produces.

2.2 CLASSIFICATION OF DRUGS

You may be used to the definition of a drug as being any substance which alters bodily function. This very general definition covers a wide range of substances, for example, antibiotics, herbal remedies, tranquillizers, tobacco and heroin.

You can probably think of a number of different ways in which drugs could be classified.

Some examples of simple classification might include:

● those which can only be obtained by medical prescription, and those which may be freely bought over a chemist's counter

● those which are legal, and those which are illicit

● those drugs which are synthetic, and those which are derived from naturally occurring substances.

You will almost certainly reflect that whether a drug is only available on prescription or may be more widely obtained has much to do with custom and tradition within a particular country.

Drugs which are sold over the counter in some countries are restricted to doctors' prescription in others.

ACTIVITY 2.1
'UNDERSTANDING DRUG USE'

Spend 20 minutes on this activity.

You should now read the Reader article 'Understanding drug use' by Cox *et al.* This article discusses in more detail the concept of drugs and drug use, in particular the definitions and sources of psychoactive drugs.

In this course we will be focussing almost exclusively on psychoactive drugs, that is, drugs which act on the brain to produce changes in mood or psychological functioning. They are taken essentially to change the way we feel.

As you are reading this article you should pay particular attention to the discussion about the different ways that drugs can be classified.

Comment

The article emphasizes the ways in which it is possible to produce multiple classifications of many drugs. Often they have multiple effects, and can have more than one site of action. For example, heroin relieves pain and affects mood, but can also constrict the pupils and slow the activity of the bowel causing constipation.

Drugs can be classified simply in terms of effects on the workings of the body, or in terms of legal status, whether they grow naturally or are refined, or how they are normally taken or absorbed. Classifications adopted depend on viewpoint and likely usage, for example, a doctor, a policeman and a user will have very different perceptions of certain drugs and therefore will use different means of classifying them.

ACTIVITY 2.2
KEEPING A DIARY OF DRUG USE

This activity is a major activity and will involve you in making a diary for two weeks regarding your own use of drugs or stimulants (tea, coffee, chocolate, sweets, cigarettes, aspirins etc.).

The basic idea is in the first of the two weeks to simply keep a note of the drugs, tablets or stimulants that you normally use, and how these make you feel. During the second week we want you to try to go without these things!

It may not be possible or practical for you to undertake such an extensive activity at this time, but we hope that you will be able to consider doing this activity in the very near future. If you are unable to do it right now then you should set a date when it will be possible to start.

It may be worth doing this activity at the same time as another member of your team, or some other colleague doing this course. Comparing and contrasting notes will be of enormous help when considering the way in which you use these substances.

Week 1

During this first week we want you to note down the times that you use any drug or stimulant. For most people this will be tobacco, alcohol or tea and coffee. Others may have a tendency to rush for chocolate bars when in need of a bit of a boost. Any people doing the course who are taking prescribed drugs, sleeping tablets etc., should also enter these in their diary.

Each time that you 'use' and make an entry in your chart consider:

● What do you feel like before taking it?
● What do you feel like after taking it?
● Are there any special reasons why you are taking it at this particular time . . . frustration, habit, boredom, feeling low?

Week 2

During the second week of the activity try to avoid the use of the drugs and stimulants that you have been keeping a note of for the preceding week. This will not be possible for everybody (obviously diabetics should continue to take their insulin, and any other people taking the course who are on prescribed drugs that must not be stopped, should continue to take them). But remember that many of you who are trying to help drug users will be asking them to do something that is as hard as this activity, or even harder.

Giving up your stimulants, props, comforts and pleasures is really difficult. Completing this activity as diligently as you can possibly manage will certainly help you to make full use of the later sections which are concerned with treatment and interventions.

For each day that you manage to keep off your own particular substances (cigarettes, lunchtime pint or strong coffee) make some brief notes about how you feel.

● What do you feel like in general?
● Which times of the day are most difficult?
● If you did succumb, what made you weaken?

Comment

Looking back over the two weeks in which you have been keeping your diaries may well help you to see the patterns that you have developed in the use of certain substances.

There may have been certain times when you felt an intense craving for caffeine in some form, or really couldn't do without that drink or the usual cigarette. You may have just felt generally 'not yourself' or jittery, or developed physical symptoms such as headaches.

One of our testers for this course commented, 'Yes it was good to get back to caffeine after my days in OU imposed hell!' Others recognized particularly difficult times to continue abstaining from alcohol, for example, 'refused drinks at a party all night . . . made to *feel* the problem as well as think it.' Some found alternatives to tea and coffee and suggested herbal teas and alcohol-free lager.

We hope that this exercise will help you not to underestimate the task that we might be expecting others to perform when asking them, or helping them, to break their usual habits.

Never underestimate the importance and strength of habit. It is very difficult to avoid going back to drug taking however strong the initial resolve.

2.3 SET AND SETTING

The effects of any drug will be influenced by many attributes of the drug itself, its pharmacology or mode of chemical action, by the dose, as well as by the size and constitution of the user.

However, external influences are also very important, notably the psychological *set* of the user and the *setting* in which the drug is taken.

SET

This is the word that is often used for the psychological set, or expectations, which are brought to a drug experience. People are rarely emotionally neutral about any drug. We all may expect to feel 'revived' by a cup of coffee, 'relaxed' by a gin and tonic, and so on. Experiments have shown that for many drugs the *anticipated* effect is so strong that changes in mood and behaviour can be provoked equally by a disguised placebo as by the drug itself. Vuchinich *et al.* (1979), for instance, found that being told that alcohol was being consumed, even when this was not the case, induced more mirth and conviviality amongst drinkers than was produced by alcohol itself.

SETTING

The effect of any drug is also strongly influenced by the setting, or environment, in which it is taken. For example, the good humour of a party may be more potent than the pharmacology of the drug itself. With cannabis, the effect of the experience appears to be strongly influenced by the mood of the occasion.

ACTIVITY 2.3
SET AND SETTING
(Activity 2 on audio)
Spend 25 minutes on this activity.

Listen to the short taped extracts of people talking about the way they use drugs. The extracts are with people who use opiates or alcohol. As you are listening you should note down why you think the person takes the particular drug, and what effect is desired from taking it.

Consider also the user's psychological set and the setting in which the drug is taken.

How influential do you think that the set and setting are in the use of drugs by these people?

Comment

It is apparent that for some people taking drugs is a very social activity. It is part of the social scene to which they belong, and alcohol or drugs 'oil the wheels' of the interactions between people. For other people, maybe with more problems in controlling their habit, drug use becomes a more solitary activity.

2.4 HOW PEOPLE TAKE DRUGS

The *route of administration* is very important in influencing the rapidity with which the drug reaches the brain. The common routes are swallow (oral), smoke, sniff and shoot (injection).

DRUG DOSAGE

The effect of any drug is, of course, also related to the dose taken. However, doubling the dose does not necessarily double the effect. The relationship between dose and effect is somewhat more complex. A small dose may have little effect, then a threshold is reached and the impact of successive doses grows quite rapidly until a ceiling, or upper limit is reached, after which increasing dosage may produce little further impact.

The effect of a given dose will also depend on the form in which the drug is taken and the route of administration.

A glass of whisky, which contains alcohol in a very concentrated form, will have more immediate effect on blood alcohol levels than a comparable amount of alcohol in a more dilute medium such as beer or wine.

PURITY

Many modern drugs are extracted from, or synthesized versions of, plants. In their original form these substances are much less potent, because the active ingredient is only a small part of the whole. For example, opium is much less potent than its derivative heroin, and cocaine is far stronger than coca leaves.

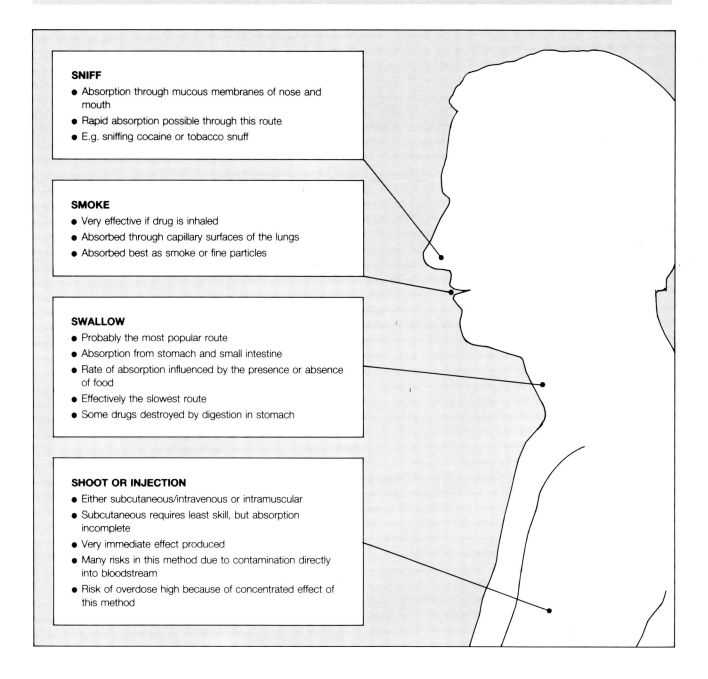

SNIFF
- Absorption through mucous membranes of nose and mouth
- Rapid absorption possible through this route
- E.g. sniffing cocaine or tobacco snuff

SMOKE
- Very effective if drug is inhaled
- Absorbed through capillary surfaces of the lungs
- Absorbed best as smoke or fine particles

SWALLOW
- Probably the most popular route
- Absorption from stomach and small intestine
- Rate of absorption influenced by the presence or absence of food
- Effectively the slowest route
- Some drugs destroyed by digestion in stomach

SHOOT OR INJECTION
- Either subcutaneous/intravenous or intramuscular
- Subcutaneous requires least skill, but absorption incomplete
- Very immediate effect produced
- Many risks in this method due to contamination directly into bloodstream
- Risk of overdose high because of concentrated effect of this method

Purified or manufactured drugs have many advantages over drugs in their raw form. They contain a dose which is accurately known and does not contain other ingredients which may be unknown, or active in some other, unpredictable way. Street drugs are often contaminated with impurities or additives.

Purity is particularly crucial when a substance is being injected. Contaminants can, of course, introduce infection when substances have not been properly sterilized. There is also the danger from improperly dissolved substances lodging in the blood vessels of the brain and other parts of the body causing thrombosis and sudden death.

ACTIVITY 2.4
'THE INFECTIVE COMPLICATIONS OF DRUG MISUSE'

Spend 20 minutes on this activity.

You should now read 'The infective complications of drug misuse' by Dr Ray Brettle in the Reader. In this article Dr Brettle describes the infections associated with the intravenous use of drugs. The majority of the article is concerned with the HIV (AIDS) epidemic, and describes the necessary management of AIDS infection and preventive measures necessary to avoid its further spread.

Aids infection, and the fear of it, has become a major component in the work of people helping drug users. As you read this article you should consider how you go about keeping yourself up-to-date with the latest information and advice about the spread of this infection, and the ways in which you can help drug users avoid this particular problem.

TOLERANCE

As we become familiar with taking a particular drug we often find that we can take larger doses with less effect than we would have found at first. This process is known as *tolerance*. It is a key concept in understanding the development of dependence. The exact basis of this phenomenon is not fully understood. It may be explained partially in psychological terms – the user learns to handle the drug and becomes familiar with its effects, which no longer cause surprise. In addition to this *psychological* adaptation, *biological* tolerance also can develop.

This central nervous system adapts to reduce the effect that the drug has on the brain cells. In some instances the body also becomes more efficient in metabolizing the drug so that it is broken down and eliminated more rapidly. As a consequence of these effects the user finds he or she can take very large doses which might even kill the metabolically inexperienced user. Detoxification units for habitual drunken offenders who have developed a high degree of tolerance for alcohol have often found that these patients walk around and behave coherently with blood alcohol levels that would render most average drinkers unconscious.

'A man was brought in by the police to a casualty department. He had been in a fight in a pub and had lacerated his hand. He was clearly under the influence of alcohol but quite able to walk, albeit a little unsteadily. His speech was slurred but coherent. His blood alcohol was noted to be 500 mg%.'

'A young dock worker was admitted to the same casualty department as an emergency. He had been found unconscious in his flat by friends. They had been at a party, he had drunk more than one bottle of vodka and innumerable beers during the course of the evening. His blood alcohol was found to be 480 mg%. He was profoundly unconscious, he required intensive care and resuscitation in hospital and would almost certainly have died had his friends not discovered him. His friends pointed out that they had had a big win on the horses that day and they had all been celebrating. Later he admitted he was not used to drinking very large quantities of alcohol because he could not afford it.'

Comment

The first patient had acquired tolerance over many years of habitual drinking while the latter had no tolerance and his nervous system was seriously depressed by a large dose of alcohol taken within a short period of time.

Tolerance is lost after a period of abstinence. This may have important consequences for the unwary drug taker. For example, a heroin dependant person who had spent three years drug free in prison was given a fix of heroin by friends shortly after release. He took his 'usual dose' but his tolerance had been lost and it proved sufficient to put him into a coma from which he never recovered.

CROSS TOLERANCE

The adaptation to one drug often extends to other related drugs which use similar metabolic routes in the body. For instance, a middle-aged businessman was admitted to hospital for a gall-bladder operation. The anaesthetist could not understand why he found it so difficult to anaesthetise the patient. He required a very large dose of anaesthetic and took a long time to recover afterwards.

It was only later that the doctors discovered that he drank a bottle of whisky on most days and had developed tolerance which extended to related drugs including some anaesthetics.

DEPENDENCE AND WITHDRAWAL

As tolerance develops, the drug user becomes both physically and psychologically dependent on the drug. *Physical dependence* is a state in which the body has adjusted to the presence of a drug, so that when the drug is withdrawn there are clear physical withdrawal symptoms usually involving discomfort and pain (Cox *et al.*, 1983). These withdrawal symptoms are usually mild, but may be associated with fits and delirium. These serious sequelae are particularly common when withdrawing from depressant drugs such as barbiturates or alcohol.

ACTIVITY 2.5
'BENZODIAZEPINE WITHDRAWAL'

Spend about 20 minutes on this activity.

More recently the symptoms suffered by people withdrawing from long-term minor tranquillizer use has become more apparent. Read 'Benzodiazepine withdrawal' by Heather Ashton in the Reader. This is an article reporting a study which has followed up 50 patients as they have been withdrawn from taking benzodiazepines (minor tranquillizers like Valium or Ativan).

As you are reading it you should note the ways in which the withdrawal symptoms themselves can mimic the very anxiety and other symptoms that lead to the minor tranquillizers being prescribed in the first place.

Comment

Psychological dependence is associated with a craving for the effects which the drug produced and a sensed compulsion to continue using the drug, often at considerable personal cost. Deprived of the psychologically rewarding effects of the habit, the user feels almost as if he or she had suffered a bereavement. Although the symptoms attendant on withdrawal from physical dependence may be very distressing they are commonly short-lived, whereas overcoming the cravings and longings associated with psychological dependence can be much more difficult.

Immediate acute effects

These effects may become immediately apparent when a drug is used. The effects may be physical and in turn lead to social, legal or psychological problems. They may also be harmful as a result of intoxification or impaired judgement, or the user may overdose.

Long-term consequences

Harmful effects may also arise from regular hazardous use over a period of time. In addition to dependency, the excessive drinker, for example, may suffer liver disease, brain damage, loss of employment and domestic breakdown. These harmful results of drug use may occur without the user ever experiencing physical dependence.

ACTIVITY 2.6
'DRUG ABUSE BRIEFING'

Spend about 15 minutes on this activity.

Some drugs such as heroin can produce biological dependence very quickly, while others, such as cannabis seem to have only a limited ability to do this.

Some, such as LSD, are more unpredictable in even a single dose, while others like tobacco have devastating longer-term consequences for health.

Now read the extract from the introduction to the ISDD 'Drug Abuse Briefing' in the Reader.

In this extract on drug terms and drug taking and risk taking you will find further details of the points that we have covered so far in this section of the course.

As you are reading the article you should remember the ways in which drug problems can arise: intoxication, dependence, and so on.

How a problem is defined is very much influenced by who is identifying it, in what circumstances the definition is developed and what purpose might be served by defining the problem. Although there might be less controversy about the effects of drug use the identification of some of these effects as 'problems' clearly raises many problems. We look at this issue in more detail in Activity 2.7.

ACTIVITY 2.7
USING A DRUG EFFECTS CHECKLIST
(Activity 3 on audio)

You should spend 25 minutes on this activity.

(a) Listen to the extract on the audio cassette of Carl talking about the various problems he has encountered as a result of taking drugs. As you are listening to this you should have the drug effects checklist open in front of you. As the story continues you should make a note of the problems that have been encountered and decide from the checklist into which category you think the various problems might fall.

Keep your notes from this activity for use with Activity 3.3 which also refers to this extract on the audio cassette.

(b) You should now try to think of someone you have had contact with who has recently had a series of problems associated with drug usage.

Make a list of the problems that have been encountered and analyse these using the checklist.

Drug effects checklist

When considering a harmful drug effect you should always try to keep the following questions in mind:

● Is the effect due to the pharmocologically active ingredients of the drug?

● Is the effect due principally to the route of administration, or the presence of impurities?

● Is the effect due to withdrawal of the drug rather than its presence?

● Is the effect due to an overdose or does it occur at normal dosage?

● Is the effect strongly determined by the user's personality or environment (set or setting)?

● Is the effect due to the attitude of society towards this drug or this user?

● Is the effect due to neglect of other needs caused by the investment of the user's energy and finance in maintaining the drug habit?

Comment

The concept of 'problem' is, of course, relative to circumstances – a problem in whose eyes? The decision to categorize a drug as illegal renders *all* use a problem irrespective of the effects of the drug itself on that user. Being arrested is undoubtedly harmful, with short-term distress and inconvenience and maybe considerable long-term consequences. For example, employment prospects may be badly affected.

A problem may be more evident to those around than to the user. For example, a wife may worry about her husband smoking – she is irritated by the smell of tobacco, concerned about her enforced passive smoking and its consequences for the children, annoyed by his morning cough and concerned that he will develop lung cancer or die from a heart attack. She repeatedly asks him to stop smoking. From his perspective he might say that she nags and is anti-smoking – it doesn't worry him, and what he does to his own body is his own affair.

The effects of drugs clearly cannot be reduced to a single list of substances and their actions. The following section of the course concerns classification. It is inevitably a simplification of what you are by now well aware is a very complex issue.

2.5 PSYCHOACTIVE DRUGS

Most psychoactive drugs can be placed within a general classification in terms of their effects. They can in most cases be classified as *depressants, stimulants, hallucinogens* or *narcotics*.

Some drugs such as cannabis and tobacco do not fit very easily into this classification.

As you go through this section of the course and follow the selected examples of the different types of drugs you will become more familiar with the general characteristics of each category.

DEPRESSANTS

Alcohol, tranquillizers, sleeping tablets (hypnotics), anaesthetics and volatile solvents sniffed as glues, seem at first sight to be a very mixed bag of different substances. They are, however, all depressants of the central nervous system. In a small dose they produce a calming or relaxing effect, and as the dose increases this gives way to a feeling of drowsiness and sleep. Tolerance develops to all of these substances, and to a varying degree they also produce psychological and physical dependence. Once dependence is fully established, then withdrawal symptoms are commonly very severe and protracted.

To help you consider the range of effects of all depressant drugs, we shall concentrate on alcohol as a typical example. It is the best known and most widely abused of all these substances.

Alcohol

Alcohol (ethanol or ethyl alcohol) has been used and abused since prehistoric times, occurring as the product of a natural fermentation of fruit juice or grain. Around AD 800 distillation was discovered.

The short-term effects of alcohol depend on the dose taken, the tolerance which the drinker has developed, and the drinker's body weight. Women are more sensitive to comparable doses of alcohol than are men, because they have a relatively greater percentage of fat in their body, and thus have a smaller body water component in which the alcohol will dissolve. A given dose of alcohol produces a 25–30% higher concentration in the blood of a woman than a man even after the body weight of the woman is taken into account.

Alcohol is absorbed into the body through the stomach and intestines, and distributed throughout the body by the blood stream. In pregnant women, alcohol, like other drugs, crosses the placental barrier to reach the developing baby.

Alcohol causes the pulse to quicken, the blood vessels of the skin to dilate, and the resulting flush produces a feeling of warmth. In consequence it is a potent cause of heat loss from the skin. This may have fatal consequences in hypothermia for the elderly and individuals exposed to severe weather. Hypothermia is a real hazard to the drunk who collapses and sleeps rough overnight. This is one example of a drug having a number of different sites of action.

We don't drink to produce dilation of the blood vessels, any more than the heroin abuser uses that drug to produce constipation. These effects are peripheral to the main reason for use. Side effects of this kind may be important and damaging.

The main reason for taking alcohol is for its effect on the brain. The relationship between particular doses and behavioural consequences are shown in the diagram opposite. As the blood alcohol level rises, progressively more functions of the brain are affected. At high concentrations the nervous system is depressed and the drinker falls asleep and becomes unconscious. The basic vital functions of the brain in maintaining breathing and circulation are eventually suppressed and death follows.

HOW DOES ALCOHOL AFFECT PHYSICAL AND MENTAL BEHAVIOUR?

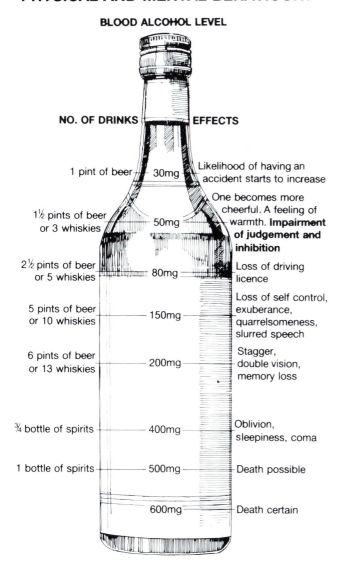

BLOOD ALCOHOL LEVEL

NO. OF DRINKS		EFFECTS
1 pint of beer	30mg	Likelihood of having an accident starts to increase
1½ pints of beer or 3 whiskies	50mg	One becomes more cheerful. A feeling of warmth. **Impairment of judgement and inhibition**
2½ pints of beer or 5 whiskies	80mg	Loss of driving licence
5 pints of beer or 10 whiskies	150mg	Loss of self control, exuberance, quarrelsomeness, slurred speech
6 pints of beer or 13 whiskies	200mg	Stagger, double vision, memory loss
¾ bottle of spirits	400mg	Oblivion, sleepiness, coma
1 bottle of spirits	500mg	Death possible
	600mg	Death certain

The Story of James

James Geddes, a 16 year old, went on holiday to Spain. While there he met a friend and they engaged in a drinking contest. He was keen to prove that the Scots could drink more than the French or Germans. He downed a bottle and a half of brandy to prove this point, collapsed into unconsciousness, was placed on his bed by friends and was found dead in the morning.

Health consequences of alcohol misuse

Intoxication/acute effects	Chronic excess
Alcoholic poisoning	Physical and psychological dependence
Acute gastritis	
Diarrhoea	Cognitive impairment
Hangover symptoms	Wernicke's encephalopathy
Amnesia	
Hypoglycaemia	Korsakow's syndrome
Cerebrovascular accidents	Peripheral neuropathy
	Fatty liver
Cardiac arrhythmia ('holiday heart syndrome')	Hepatitis
	Cirrhosis (30% are excessive drinkers)
Foetal damage	Carcinoma of liver
Impotence	Pancreatitis (acute and 50% chronic)
Accidents	
Head injury	Irritable bowel syndrome
Suicide attempts	Hypertension
	Cardiomyopathy
	Obesity
	Cushing's syndrome
	Diabetes
	Testicular atrophy
	Impotence
	Foetal alcohol syndrome
	Carcinoma of the mouth, larynx and oesophagus

Note:
32% of patients attending Accident and Emergency departments have blood alcohol levels above 80 mg%

42% of patients with serious head injuries are intoxicated

49% of drivers killed in RTA are intoxicated

Hypnotics

Hypnotics and depressant drugs are very widely prescribed by doctors and are very widely abused.

There are a wide variety of sleeping tablets available which have different durations of action. To varying degrees they all possess similar tendencies to produce tolerance and dependence. The user finds that he or she has to take an increasing dose to maintain the desired sleep pattern, and finds on giving up the drug that insomnia returns and it may take several months before a more natural sleep rhythm is restored.

The extent to which tolerance and subsequent dependence develops is related to the dose and also to the particular form of the hypnotic used. Clinical studies show that in most cases a degree of physical dependence can be established within one month of regular use.

The chronic abuser appears drowsy, speech is slurred and poor co-ordination increases the likelihood of accidents. Essentially he or she appears drunk, but there is no smell of alcohol. The most commonly abused type of hypnotics are the barbiturates.

Following abrupt withdrawal of barbiturates, the user experiences a rebound sleeplessness, tremor, restlessness and irritability, very similar to the withdrawal symptoms experienced by the person who has become alcohol dependent. Epileptic fits are particularly common during barbiturate withdrawal and in one series occurred in 75% of cases. Delirium is also quite common during withdrawal.

Young people often abuse barbiturates and other hypnotics and tranquillizers to obtain a relaxed, disinhibited feeling. In some parts of the country they are cheaper than alcohol and may be taken to produce a similar drunken state. They are also used along with stimulants to calm the user down from the aroused state induced by some other drugs. Intravenous use of barbiturate is quite common, often amongst established heroin users, taken as an alternative to opiates. When used in this way it is a common cause of death due to respiratory depression.

Tranquillizers

Approximately 1 in 7 British adults take tranquillizers at some time during the year and 1 in 40 take them more regularly.

Most people who are dependent on tranquillizers have been started on them by doctors, although there is a sizeable black market and considerable informal swapping of these drugs. Many people are introduced to them by friends who may have kept some in the drug cupboard from a previous prescription. The most widely used tranquillizers are Librium, Valium and Ativan but there are many other variations on these. Most of them have a common chemical structure (called benzodiazepine).

Tranquillizers produce relaxation and lower anxiety. They are effective in dosages which don't usually cause drowsiness. Nonetheless, in common with other central nervous system depressants, they will produce drowsiness and sleep if taken in a large enough dose. Their effects are, of course, exacerbated by adding another central nervous system depressant, such as alcohol.

Tolerance and dependence develop after three or four months usage even at a modest therapeutic dose.

You will remember from the Reader article by Ashton, which you studied earlier in this section, about the particular problems caused by withdrawal from this type of drug.

It is estimated that there are at least one hundred thousand people dependant on tranquillizers in Britain. It is also certainly true that very many more women are dependent on tranquillizers than men.

Solvent abuse (glue sniffing)

This subject is mentioned here because all the inhaled substances are in fact central nervous system depressants. The vapour must be deeply inhaled to produce the desired effect. Inhalation of drugs in this way is not a new phenomenon: nitrous oxide (laughing gas) was widely abused in the last century. It was investigation of this form of drug that led to the discovery of anaesthetics. The principal cause of concern at present is episodic outbreaks of solvent abuse, usually by children in their early teens. It is a good example of drug taking occurring by imitation and demonstrates the importance of friends in influencing fashion. When details about these drugs and their means of administration have been widely publicized, young people have often been attracted to try them, and a group of friends will start a mini-epidemic, in a school or an area, which usually dies out as they mature.

Such drugs may produce sores and ulcers around the nose and mouth. They also may cause damage to the liver, kidneys and brain. The effects are rarely fatal, but deaths, when they have occurred, arise as a consequence of heart failure or respiratory failure due to the bronchi going into spasm and preventing air reaching the lungs. This is particularly liable to occur when an aerosol is blown directly into the mouth and inhaled. Other deaths arise because of accidents occurring while the user is intoxicated and through incorrect procedures leading to asphyxiation by placing the plastic bag over the head.

These hazards present a dilemma to those who are trying to prevent problems with solvent abuse. The basic dilemma is whether to tell people how to use these potentially harmful substances as safely as possible, or whether this, in itself, will be considered to be tacit approval by the authorities for young people to go ahead and experiment with them.

You will be able to study this debate in much greater detail in later sections of the course.

STIMULANTS

These drugs increase arousal and make the user feel temporarily more euphoric, alert and wide awake. Unlike hypnotics and tranquillizers they are of limited medical use and are now rarely prescribed. Amphetamines were widely prescribed at one time as appetite suppressants for obesity, but their potential for abuse caused doctors in Britain to introduce a voluntary restriction on prescribing with a consequent reduction in the level of availability and misuse.

Stimulants such as *amphetamine* and *cocaine* may help the user combat tiredness, and appear to accelerate thought and speech. Appetite is suppressed, blood pressure raised, pupils dilated, the user appears tremulous, pale, jittery and keyed up. A degree of tolerance develops quite quickly with pure cocaine and amphetamines and the user soon finds that he or she is requiring increasing doses to obtain the desired 'high'.

Biological dependence and withdrawal phenomena are less evident, but the user quickly becomes psychologically dependent on the euphoria which the drugs produce, and also requires the drug to combat the troughs of depression and despair which often occur on the morning after use.

Tolerant individuals may soon be taking very high doses and it is usually in these circumstances that mental breakdowns (psychoses) occur. Some users develop delusions of persecution and become fearful and aggressive to those around, misinterpreting actions and developing a paranoid view of their surroundings.

Amphetamines can be taken intravenously which accentuates the effects obtained, and multiplies the hazards.

Cocaine is derived from the leaves of *Erythroxylum coca* trees. The peasants in the mountains where the trees grow have for centuries chewed these leaves to help them cope with their harsh conditions of work. The drug in purified form can be taken by mouth, smoked, sniffed or injected. If cocaine hydrochloride is converted to its base commonly called 'crack', it can be heated and the fumes inhaled. This is a highly effective means of obtaining a very intense and immediate effect from the drug and this 'free basing' has become increasingly common. Cocaine was widely used last century. Freud was an enthusiastic user and an advocate of its powers. It was also present in a number of potions and tonics such as the original Coca-Cola. The cocaine from all these products has now been withdrawn and supplies of cocaine are largely confined to a flourishing black market.

Caffeine – found in coffee, tea, cocoa, chocolate, cola drinks and some non prescription headache medications – is the most widely used psychoactive drug in the world. It is a mild stimulant and also produces a moderate rise in pulse and blood pressure and general arousal, causing insomnia for some individuals. High daily dosages (such as six cups of coffee i.e. 600 mg of caffeine) can induce agitation, tremor, nervousness, insomnia and irregularities of the heart rhythm.

Remember that caffeine is a stimulant

Dose	Caffeine
cup of brewed or percolated coffee	100mg
cup of medium strength tea	30mg
can of cola drink	30mg
chocolate bar	25mg

Tolerance and dependence occur at high dosage and the withdrawal symptoms are characterized by severe headache, lethargy and irritability.

Some of you will have personal experience of these effects of caffeine. Those of you who have completed Activity 2.2 in which you may have attempted to go without caffeine for a week will almost certainly be able to confirm these findings of the effects of caffeine.

Nicotine is probably best classed as a mild stimulant. It is derived from the tobacco plant and is commonly taken by smoking (as cigars or cigarettes), sniffing (as snuff), or chewing, or holding next to the capillary membranes of the mouth (for example, as the recently introduced Skoal Bandits).

Tolerance and dependence develop quite rapidly and craving, nervousness and irritability are evident on withdrawal. Tobacco is a major cause of ill health particularly in causing lung cancer, bronchitis and heart disease.

In the present context, tobacco is an important example of a highly dangerous drug which is readily available.

HALLUCINOGENS

This is a rather misleading term because these drugs do not consistently give rise to hallucinations, but commonly produce disturbances of perception and a changed state of consciousness and awareness. This may produce feelings varying from terror to ecstasy. Hallucinogens include a wide variety of chemically dissimilar substances.

Some are manufactured, like LSD, and others occur naturally as plants and fungi. Some people have attributed mystical properties to these psychoactive changes and valued the insights and visions which they produce. They have very few acknowledged medicinal uses. They do not appear to produce biological dependence (although cannabis may be an exception), but tolerance and a degree of psychological dependence is common.

The hallucinations, delusions and altered perceptions which these drugs produce may prove very frightening. A 'bad-trip' is a very alarming experience and crimes and accidents have been known to occur when the user was acting under delusions induced by the drug.

As many as 25 per cent of users of hallucinogens will experience a transient return of the hallucinatory and delusional experience weeks or months after the drug has been taken. The episode is usually brief lasting seconds or minutes but it is often frightening and disturbing. The cause of this strange phenomenon is not known.

Cannabis is usually classified as a hallucinogen because it alters perception − particularly the sense of time. Tolerance has been demonstrated both in humans and animals. Withdrawal symptoms have not been unequivocally demonstrated. Regular users may become psychologically dependent (Maykut, 1985).

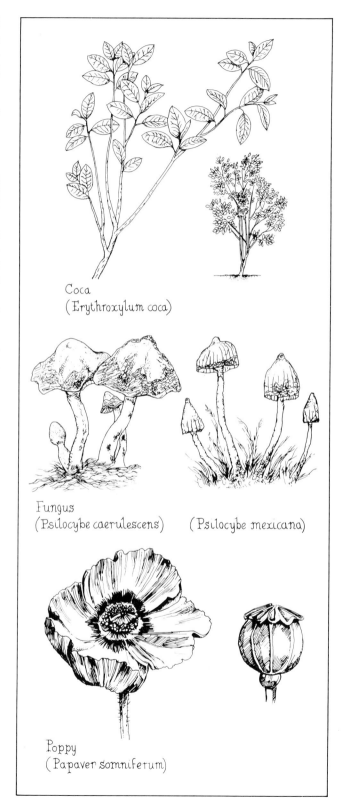

Coca
(Erythroxylum coca)

Fungus
(Psilocybe caerulescens)   (Psilocybe mexicana)

Poppy
(Papaver somniferum)

NARCOTICS

These drugs are powerful analgesics that produce a detached calm state of mind which can remove concerns about both physical and psychological pain. The naturally occurring opiate, morphine, is obtained by refining the crude tar-like exudate obtained from the opium poppy. Heroin is more potent than morphine and is derived from opium. They are most active and effective when given by injection. Tolerance and physical dependence develop rapidly and the withdrawal symptoms are unpleasant. They are characterized by agitation, a restless disturbed sleep, abdominal cramps, diarrhoea, watering eyes and a running nose, dilated pupils and tremor. These withdrawal symptoms last for a week or more.

Heroin addicts have a reduced life expectancy and a mortality rate 15 times higher than expected. Death is not usually due to the direct effects of the drug itself, unless as a consequence of overdose. The abuser can succumb to one of the illnesses associated with unclean injection techniques such as septicaemia, venous thrombosis, hepatitis or AIDS.

Because injection is so dangerous, many users now prefer to smoke heroin. Some heroin is placed in a strip of tin foil and heated until it gives off smoke which is inhaled. The substance writhes above the foil while it is being heated giving rise to the colourful phrase 'chasing the dragon'. Most users recognize the hazards of injection (main lining), but nonetheless may be attracted to trying this because of the intensity of the experience or 'rush' which comes with this method.

Methadone is a synthetic opiate which is much longer acting than heroin, but nonetheless addictive. It is usually taken orally as a mixture and is sometimes prescribed by clinics in maintenance therapy.

DRUG ABUSE AS A WAY OF LIFE: POLYDRUG ABUSE

You will already be well aware of the dangers of thinking purely in terms of a list of drugs matched with their effects, and of viewing drug abusers as dependent on any particular drug. Evidence suggests that many are much more dependent on a *lifestyle of which drug abuse is a part* rather than dependence on any particular drug.

The table below shows the range of drugs taken by one sample of young people in Scotland.

Drugs ever taken 'for kicks' by 72 Scottish hospital attenders (Plant, 1987)

Drug	N	Drug	N
Cannabis	51	Valium	5
Amphetamines	38	Omnopon	3
LSD	34	Cough linctuses	3
Heroin	29	Methedrine	3
Barbiturates	27	Inhalers	2
Mandrax	25	Librium	2
Morphine	22	Diconal	1
Methadone	13	Preludin	1
Opium	9	Palfrium	1
Mescalin	9	Demerol	1
Tuinal	7	Largactil	1
Cocaine	5	Solvents/glues	1

The tendency is to take whatever is available on the scene; whatever is offered by friends or can be bought in the local pub. Chemical drug dependence is in fact rare even amongst the sizeable minority who take drugs as part of their ordinary leisure activities.

Even with heroin, a drug with a very high potential for producing dependence, there are many casual users. People rarely comment that they start drugs because of a deep seated psychological need or problem, they approach them more in a spirit of experimentation and enquiry. In the following chapters we will be exploring in much more detail the reasons why people take drugs.

Many seem to take a drug simply to see what it will be like. The effect of drugs and the choice of drugs often tell us more about the users' culture, social class and background than they do about the drug itself. Availability, fashion, price and legal status all play a part in determining choice.

There is evidence that knowing the effects and the dangers of a particular drug does not prove to be a sufficient deterrent: many young people take up smoking tobacco and a majority of drinkers admit to driving while under the influence of alcohol.

Most users of illicit drugs are much more aware of their effects than are their parents, teachers or even their doctors. It seems reasonable to suppose that a basic knowledge of the actions of drugs is a necessary but not sufficient basis for offering help and understanding to those who abuse these substances.

FURTHER READING

Berridge, V. & Edwards, G. *Opium and the people,* Allen Lane, 1981

Field, T. *Escaping the dragon,* Unwin, 1985

Orford, J. *Excessive appetites,* Wiley, 1985

Picardie, J. & Wade, D. *Heroin chasing the dragon,* Penguin, 1985

Royal College of Psychiatrists *Alcohol: our favourite drug,* Tavistock, 1986

Tyler, A. *Street drugs,* New English Library, 1986

Weil, A. *The natural mind,* Penguin, 1972

REFERENCES

Cox, T.M., Jacobs, M.R., Leblanc, A.E. & Marshman, J.A. (1983) *Drugs and drug abuse,* Addiction Research Foundation, Toronto

Maykut, M.O. (1985) 'Health consequences of acute and chronic marijuana use', *Prog. Neuro-Psychopharmacol. and Biol. Psychiat.* 9(3): pp. 209–38

Plant, M.A. (1987) *Drugs in perspective,* Hodder and Stoughton

Vuchinich, R.E., Tucker, J.A. & Sobell, M.B. (1979) 'Alcohol, expectancy, cognitive labelling and mirth' *Journal of Abnormal Psychol.* Dec., 88(6) pp. 641–51

3 DRUG USE AND MISUSE

3.1 INTRODUCTION

There is enormous diversity in the variety and forms of drug use and in this chapter we not only look at who might use, or misuse, drugs but we concentrate on the context in which drugs are consumed. The emphasis here is that an examination of the social context in which drugs are introduced and consumed can provide us with the background for understanding the lifestyle of drug users. The chapter looks at the use of drugs firmly within their social and cultural contexts. It is these contexts which will invariably offer the initial encouragement for someone to try a drug, and they will also often be major obstacles for someone who wishes to stop using drugs. When drug use is set within these contexts, moreover, then we can examine what is common in the experiences which people have with otherwise quite different pharmacological agents. Pharmacology is not unimportant to our understanding of drug use and misuse, but it is, most crucially, the social contexts which seem to shape definitions of acceptable 'drug use' as against unacceptable 'drug misuse'.

3.2 VARIETIES OF CONTEXTS AND FORMS OF DRUG USE

In order to identify some beliefs about the social and cultural contexts of drug use and also the kinds of people who use (or misuse) drugs we will look at two case studies. The first is concerned with the extent to which young people use drugs and the drugs which young people use. The second case study looks at alcohol use, the drug with which most people are familiar, although it is unlikely that any individual will be familiar with all the social contexts where alcohol is consumed.

THE ACCENT ON YOUTH

In most public discussions on drugs it is usually adolescents who are thought of as the group most 'at risk'. But why is this? On any count, it is a strange assumption, because most drug use, together with the harmful effects of misuse, is concentrated among the adult population. The average age of people admitted as in-patients for alcohol dependence, for example, is 40 years. The vast majority of people who are dependent on tobacco are also adults, and young people are, in fact, less likely to smoke than their parents. The problems of dependence on medically prescribed drugs are also found overwhelmingly among middle-aged and elderly people. This problem is one which has been neglected until very recently, even though there are approximately one million people (including a disproportionate number of women) who are receiving prescriptions for mood-changing drugs such as the so-called 'benzodiazepines' (Librium, Valium, etc.). It is estimated that one-tenth will become dependent (Lacey & Woodward, 1985).

However, public discussion on 'drugs' does not usually focus on alcohol, tobacco or medically prescribed 'tranquillizers'. It is more likely to be concerned with solvents, cannabis, heroin, and the opiates, amphetamines, LSD and hallucinogenic mushrooms, etc. Cannabis is certainly a widely used drug in contemporary Britain, with some estimates suggesting that there might be two million daily users with as many as ten million people having tried the drug, in spite of legal prohibition (Malyon, 1985). However, if we set cannabis to one side, illicit drugs are only used by a tiny proportion of the population compared with alcohol, tobacco and 'tranquillizers'. Moreover, with the exception of solvents, these illicit drugs are also undoubtedly more widely used by adults or young adults than by people of school age. The association between young people and drugs is therefore largely a myth.

Having said this, certain forms of drug use might start early in a person's life even though they only become a problem much later. Tobacco smoking, for example, is a habit which starts young and therefore attention to smoking among young people might prove crucial in any attempt to cut smoking habits. The major drug-related threat to life among young people, in fact, is road accidents. In 1980, for example, there were 267 deaths overall among the 15–19 age group in Scotland, of whom seven were recorded as somehow drug-related – whereas more than 200 of these deaths were due to road accidents, many of which would have been alcohol related (Plant *et al.*, 1985, p 13).

It is always necessary to keep this sense of balance when thinking about young people and drugs. But what drugs do young people actually use and what problems are associated with them? This question will be approached by summarizing some of the findings from a recent survey, conducted by Martin Plant and his colleagues in a region of Scotland, which studied the self-reported drug use among a sample of school-leavers who were then followed up a few years later when they were 19–20 years old.

Almost two-thirds of the group did not smoke tobacco, with slightly more girls than boys admitting to smoking at the age of 15–16 years. There was almost no change in this proportion of non-smokers when the group were followed up four years later. This reinforces the view that smoking is a habit which starts early. By contrast 98 per cent of the 15–16 year olds had tasted alcohol,

although slightly less than half the males reported that they had had a drink during the previous week and only one-third of the females. Four years later only a quarter of the females said that they had not had a drink during the previous week, compared to a mere 13 per cent of the young men. The average amount of alcohol consumed by the males also increased substantially as they got older, athough interestingly it had not changed among young women.

We can already see, then, that when thinking about drug use it is important to keep a clear distinction between the sexes. There is very little research on these gender differences, but it would appear that they can sometimes be significant in shaping drug choices. In Plant's study, for example, it was clear that young men and women not only drink different amounts of alcohol, but they also drank in different company and on different occasions. There were few differences in this respect among school-leavers, but when they were older the young men were much more likely to drink in the company of friends of the same sex, whereas young women were slightly more likely to drink with friends or relatives in their own homes or in the home of a friend. Bearing in mind that women will sometimes be made to feel unwelcome in public places for drinking, the tendency for women to drink in the home might be established quite early in life.

As far as illicit drugs were concerned, the only real 'competitor' to alcohol and tobacco was cannabis. Among the school-leavers approximately seven per cent of both sexes had tried cannabis and five per cent had experimented with solvents, whereas for all other illicit drugs the proportion who had tried them was never much more than one per cent and often less. By the time of the follow-up study, however, one-third of young men had tried cannabis and almost a quarter of young women. As many young men, therefore, had smoked cannabis as were tobacco smokers, although, of course, this does not mean that they smoked cannabis daily. Experience with amphetamines has also increased among young men to nearly six per cent, whereas solvent use had dropped away to an insignificant level among this older age group. Otherwise, there was no noticeable change in any other category of illicit drug use. Whereas overall one-quarter of the 19–20 year olds reported that they had at some time used illicit drugs, this was overwhelmingly limited to cannabis and amphetamines, and even then mainly on a very occasional basis.

This study, together with similar findings from other research, shows that frequent illicit drug use is extremely rare among young people even when they have left school and had more opportunity to experiment. It 'offers further confirmation', the authors say, 'that most illicit drug use is not regular and does not involve self-reported problems. Only a tiny minority of those who had used illicit drugs reported having experienced harm thereby or being daily drug users. These conclusions are quite conventional, but are worth emphasising in view of the high level of public concern that youthful drug use provokes' (Plant et al., 1985, p. 83).

The next question that needs to be asked, however, is whether particular groups of young people are more likely to experiment with drugs, or to develop drug-related problems. Plant's study established a number of broad groupings. Young men from lower-class homes reported drinking significantly more than those from higher-class backgrounds, for example, although social class made no difference to female drinking habits. The study found no relationship between unemployment and alcohol consumption, although unemployment did increase the likelihood that both sexes would experiment with illicit drugs. The most likely predictor that either sex would use illicit drugs, however, was heavy alcohol consumption, with tobacco smoking close behind. The study also examined family background and found that those brought up either by their mother or father alone were no more likely to have used Category A drugs (e.g. heroin or cocaine) than anyone else.

On the basis of this and other research work, we can say that if there is an 'at risk' group of young people then it is those who consume a heavy amount of the legally approved drugs, alcohol and tobacco. In practical terms this means that a key question for drug-related work with young people must be whether to focus attention on the very small group of problem drug users who emerge during school years, or to engage in more broadly targeted health education activities on the much more widely used legal drugs. Detailed examination of actual drug choice patterns among young people shows how difficult it is to make easy distinctions between legitimate 'use' and illegitimate drug 'misuse'.

The pattern of drug use which Martin Plant found in his Scottish survey conformed very closely with other national and regional surveys. It is important to note, nevertheless, that substantial local and regional variations in patterns of drug use, the drugs most commonly used, and the extent of drug use and misuse, especially where illicit drugs are concerned, can be expected. Amidst growing concern about the problem of heroin misuse, for example, recent research has shown that it is at the moment highly scattered and localized, with a tendency for the most serious problems of heroin use to be densely located in areas of high unemployment and social deprivation (Parker et al., 1986; Pearson et al., 1986).

Another way in which illicit drug use varies locally and regionally is in the vocabulary used to describe the drugs, the ways in which they are used, and their pharmacological effects. However, although you might find it useful to become familiar with local terminology, it is probably unwise to use these words oneself. You might feel that you are being friendly and accepting by using local slang, but this may be interpreted from the other side, perhaps especially with young people, as an attempt to be 'fresh' or 'clever'.

VARIETIES OF ALCOHOL CONSUMPTION

At this point we turn to a closer examination of the social contexts of drug use. When thinking of 'drug use', people tend to think that the pharmacological effects of drugs are the main reason for using them. And yet this is probably not a useful place to start, although these effects are not unimportant. It is the social contexts in which drugs are used, however, which seem to have the most important influences on why people begin and continue to use drugs. People will invariably be introduced to different forms of drug use by friends, for example, and the contexts of friendship will be the most powerful encouragements to experiment with drugs (Pearson et al., 1986; Pearson, 1987).

In order to examine these issues we will look at alcohol consumption and the different forms which it takes. Most people will be familiar with various kinds of drinking patterns, although the social contexts are so varied that none of us will be familiar with all of them. Think, for example, of what is often called 'social drinking'. The home and the public house are the most common places for drinking. The public house is, of course, a major social institution in British life but it has many different forms. There is the 'local', which will serve a regular clientele drawn from the surrounding neighbourhood. This has probably not changed a great deal since the Mass Observation (1943) study of *The Pub and the People* or, at least, the rate of change has not been as great as that in other aspects of social life in post-war Britain. Other kinds of pub, however, serve very different social functions, such as busy city centre pubs, with a transient lunchtime clientele; or those in the countryside which might be visited by day-trippers and tourists; or those which offer 'disco' type functions, where young people might be found, etc. And even in individual pubs there will often be more than one bar, maybe a 'public' bar where working men and 'regulars' gather; as against a 'saloon' bar where the clientele are somewhat different.

There are also other kinds of public places for drinking, such as clubs – working men's clubs; political clubs; 'gay' clubs; or the select 'gentlemen's' clubs of London's West End. Drinking wine with a meal, whether at home or in a restaurant, is another way of consuming alcohol. There are various forms of parties – sherry parties; office parties; and so on. Or, there are more private forms of drinking, such as when someone enjoys a drink in the early evening at home in order to signal the end of the working day. Private, or 'lone', drinking will often be disapproved of and thought to be verging on drug 'misuse', because it is 'secretive'. However, there are also familiar expressions which suggest a medicinal reason for private drinking – a 'nip to keep the cold out' or to 'help' a bad head-cold. Finally, there are disapproved public forms of drinking such as the 'skid row' culture of 'bottle gangs' in the street.

This enormous variety of social contexts for drinking will influence the meanings which people attach to drinking behaviour. Some people will typically go to a pub as a way of providing a 'change of atmosphere' and getting out of the house. Others will prefer to drink in the familiarity of their own home. Someone who enjoys a quiet glass of wine at home in the evening, for example, might think of the public house as a noisy location frequented by 'drunks' and other nuisances. Whereas someone who drinks regularly in a pub might regard drinking a bottle of wine at home in the course of the evening as somehow excessive, unsociable and 'deviant'. Some people will only drink among friends, while others will enjoy brief acquaintances in a bar.

Despite changes in the past ten years, public houses are still often decidedly male territories where women on their own will be made to feel unwelcome, if not actually defined as 'slags' or prostitutes (McConville, 1983). It might be understandable, then, if women's drinking patterns centred more on the home. However, this can lead to problematic definitions of women's drinking because of its secretive 'lone-drinking' suggestions. Finally, there is the question of the meaning given to drinking alcohol in relation to work as well as leisure. In some occupations, business negotiations will provide a context for drinking and 'hospitality'. In other occupations, drinking will be strictly prohibited.

ACTIVITY 3.1
TWO SCENARIOS: 'THE PUB' AND 'THE SHERRY PARTY'

Spend 20 minutes on this activity

Read the two scenarios of alcohol consumption below, and while you are studying these make short notes on (a) what is going on, (b) what is different about the two scenarios, and (c) what makes them similar?

The Pub

Michael Quinn had been a 'regular' at the 'Orb and Sceptre', a pub situated in a working class district of West London. He was not a 'heavy' drinker by the conventions of the public bar, but he was there most nights when he would drink a few pints of Guinness while he talked in the company of men, before returning to his flat where he lived alone. The 'Orb and Sceptre' possessed two bars: the public bar where Michael drank and the saloon bar.

One weekend in May, Michael Quinn suffered a brain haemmorhage in the street and died 24 hours later in a local hospital. That Monday evening, shortly after opening time at the 'Orb', a group of half a dozen men, all of them 'regulars', gathered around the bar and talked about Michael remembering him as a quiet and inoffensive man. It says a great deal about the kinds of conversations which typically take place among men in a pub that nobody actually knew a great deal about Michael's private life, although it was known that he had once been married. But there was nevertheless a genuine sense of grief and concern. In his mid-50s Michael's death had been quite unexpected. 'It seems such a shame,' said one man, 'he never did no one any harm.'

For another man, a fellow Irishman, Michael's death reminded him of his own brother's death from a similar cause when he had been only 33 years old. 'What is it this brain haemmorhage? Do the doctors understand it?' There was a brief layman's discussion about 'blood clots', and also that it was better to be dead than a 'cabbage'.

Another regular, something of a local 'hard man', became thoughtful amidst this discussion among the seven men. 'What a shame,' he said, 'I mean if I was to drop dead tomorrow, you'd say "There was a good bloke." But you could also say, "He was a bit of a bugger sometimes." You know what I mean? But Mick, I don't know if I'm putting this right, but he was a really nice man. I'm just glad to say that I'd met him.'

After a few minutes the conversation passed onto other things, and the occupants of the bar broke up into three groups in quiet conversation. Drinks were purchased and consumed. A game of darts began between a group of men and other people began to drift in from work. Thirty minutes later there were fourteen people in the bar. Three men sat alone at separate tables reading the evening newspaper, in much the same way that Michael Quinn might have done in the early evening. This was a typical early evening in summer. 'And Michael would have been here,' said one man who had just arrived, 'Always on a Monday this time of night . . . There's his seat, look . . . You just never know, do you?'

The Sherry Party

An official reception was arranged by a publisher in a fashionable centre of London in order to celebrate a new volume of scholarship by an elderly and distinguished university academic. By 6.30 p.m. there were nearly 400 people gathered in an imposing hall, engaged in lively conversation and drinking wine. Waitresses circulated among the gathering offering to refill glasses and there were also small snacks and nibbles of food to be eaten. Brief speeches by the author and the Secretary of State of a relevant government department, who had been a member of the same Oxford college, had been arranged.

Most of the people were unknown to each other, except professionally. When they met on occasions, if at all, it would be at official functions such as this, or at academic conferences and other kinds of professional meeting. People often shook hands as they greeted each other. 'When was it we last met? Oh yes, that dreadful Cambridge conference . . . Wasn't it absolutely boring? Who was that awful man?'

People had come from all parts of the country, many having travelled for several hours in order to be present at this prestigious event, some from as far afield as continental Europe. At first those people who either had very close professional links, or who had established close friendships over the years stood in small groups. As the evening wore on, however, they tended to disperse as people renewed fleeting acquaintanceships with more distant professional colleagues. Groups were also occasionally broken up by the organizers, in order to make brief ceremonial introductions to the distinguished author.

There was a sense that this occasion was 'a place to be seen' and perhaps it was a more profitable use of time to engage in professional introductions, which might be of future mutual benefit, than to talk over old times with friends. There were also representatives of publishers in the gathering who were anxious to learn what research various people were now engaged in. The speeches came and went. The Secretary of State was charming and the distinguished academic showed exemplary intellectual vigour and wit for his years.

Wine having been consumed in large quantities for nearly two hours, the gathering had become more voluble and groups and sub-groups seemed to shift and change with ever greater rapidity. But at around 8 o'clock, the gathering began to break up just as quickly as it had come together. And it was now that people began to reassemble in the small groups of closer friends and acquaintances. Some made arrangements to go off together for an evening meal, whereas others decided to go onto a public house where they could continue talking and drinking together. By 8.20 p.m. there was nobody left but the women who had served drinks and who were now busy clearing up.

Comment

On the surface, one might describe the two scenarios as very different, other than that alcohol was consumed on both occasions. One way of describing the differences might be between a professional or business engagement, as against one based on kinship and friendship. Even so, this will not quite do. In the 'Orb' people often discussed business and made financial arrangements, or offered the opportunity of temporary employment to a friend whom it was known 'needed the work'. Whereas at the wine reception there were people who were close friends, but who preferred to set friendship to one side for a couple of hours in order to pursue professional matters.

In both cases, it was the life and achievements of an individual that were the focus of the occasion. Nevertheless, the differences between the two settings were considerable, in terms of the kinship and neighbourhood in the 'Orb'; as against common pursuits and interest at the sherry party. In both cases alcohol consumption was a major focus of interaction, although in neither case was it the sole focus. It seems rather obvious to say that at the sherry party people were brought together by something other than alcohol. But would it not be equally true to say that it was the 'sense of occasion' which also brought people to the 'Orb'? If not, then why had people come to this particular pub and not to one of a dozen others in the neighbourhood within easy walking distance? The point is that in both scenarios we are looking not only at a drug and its consumption, but also at a social context and a social occasion.

If drug use involves a variety of social contexts, then we might usefully think of an invitation to use a drug as also an invitation to participate in a particular kind of lifestyle. One important way in which these invitations are made is through the face-to-face context of friendship. Another is through advertisements – and alcohol advertisements can tell us a great deal about what might be thought of as socially approved contexts and reasons for drinking. There are in fact varying forms of social regulation for alcohol advertising, including the guidelines on unacceptable forms of television advertisement issued by the Independent Broadcasting Authority (IBA).

ACTIVITY 3.2
THE USE AND MISUSE OF ALCOHOL ADVERTISEMENTS

Spend 15 minutes on this activity.

In this activity you are asked to look through the newspapers that we suggested you should collect at the beginning of your studies. Search through the newspapers and make a list of all the alcohol advertisements that you can find (if newspapers are not available then look through some home journals or think of some well known advertisements for alcohol that are familiar to you). Write brief notes describing the form of persuasion involved in each advertisement, as follows: (a) What kind of drinking contexts do they promote as appropriate and attractive behaviour? (b) What kinds of lifestyles do they imply? (c) What sort of motivations for drinking do they reflect and encourage? (d) What personal ambitions seem to be identified with the advertisements? And finally, (e) do they indicate any possible kind of danger associated with drinking?

Having completed this task, you should now read the short excerpt from the Independent Broadcasting Authority guidelines reproduced below, which recommended the types of advertisements which should be avoided.

Excerpt from the IBA Code of Advertising Standards and Practices; Section 34 Alcoholic Drink

(a) Liquor advertising may not be addressed particularly to the young and no one associated with drinking in an advertisement should seem to be younger than about 25. Children may not be seen or heard in an advertisement for an alcoholic drink

(b) No liquor advertisement may feature any personality whose example young people are likely to follow

(c) Advertisements may not imply that drinking is essential to social success or acceptance or that refusal is a sign of weakness

(d) Advertisements must not feature or foster immoderate drinking. This applies to the quantity of drink being consumed in the advertisement and to the act of drinking portrayed. References to buying of rounds of drinks are not acceptable

(e) Advertisements must not claim that alcohol has therapeutic qualities nor offer it expressly as a stimulant, sedative or tranquilliser. While advertisements may refer to refreshment after physical performance, they must not give any impression that performance can be improved by drink

(f) Advertisements should not place undue emphasis on the alcoholic strength of drinks

(g) Nothing in an advertisement may link drinking with driving or with the use of potentially dangerous machinery

(h) No liquor advertisement may publicise a competition

(i) Advertisements must neither claim nor suggest that any drink can contribute towards sexual success

(j) Advertisements must not suggest that regular solitary drinking is acceptable

(k) Treatments featuring special daring or toughness must not be used in a way which is likely to associate the act of drinking with masculinity.

Now spend a further five minutes checking your original list of alcohol advertisements against these guidelines, noting both points of agreement and discrepancy between what an alcohol advertisement should (or should not) look like. Write brief notes on the IBA guidelines in response to the same questions asked of you on the newspaper advertisements; for example, the motivations, lifestyles and associations which should be guarded against.

Comment

In this activity we have tried to reinforce the view that drug use is not only about drug consumption. Alcohol advertisements are not only selling a particular brand of beer, wine or spirits, they also imply a variety of lifestyles and other attractions. Advertisements typically present a range of social settings and images – the traditional pub, the fashionable garden party, the chance love affair at a disco – some of which will only be glimpsed through the television screen or the Sunday colour supplement. Even so, they help to illustrate the cultural contexts for alcohol consumption and what is thought of as appropriate and inappropriate drinking behaviour.

3.3   MOTIVATIONS, CAREERS AND CHOICES: REASONS FOR USING DRUGS

Having discussed some of the contexts and patterns of drug use, we will now turn to the reasons why people use drugs and look at motives and subsequent drug using careers. You may well be familiar with the concepts of 'motive' and 'choice' in thinking of reasons why people do things, but you may feel that the notion of 'career' in this context is rather odd, because it is something usually applied only to a person's movement through different stages of employment. However, the concept of 'career' has been found to be extremely useful in thinking about how people become progressively involved in a range of social activities, religious movements, or drug choices.

In the drugs field, a simple model for a drug-using 'career' that is sometimes used involves three major phases – initiation, continuation and cessation – with the implication that a person's motivation may change at these different levels of drug involvement.

The reasons for starting to use a drug, therefore, then deciding to continue using it, and finally to stop using it are likely to be quite different. For example, a young person might first accept a cigarette because she is offered one by a friend and wishes to do what her friends do. She might find that the cigarette makes her feel ill, in which case she might decide that 'smoking is not for her' and refuse any subsequent offers. Or she might persist with smoking and discover how to smoke without it making her ill. She might then discover that she actually enjoys smoking and continue to smoke without the encouragement of friends, or she might feel that it helps her feel 'grown up' to have a cigarette in her hand and continue to experiment for those reasons. Subsequently she might develop a dependence on nicotine, in that she feels 'edgy' if she does not smoke regularly, and a different motivation for continuing to smoke will have been established. And later, she might develop a cough which persuades her that smoking is unhealthy and decide to stop smoking. Or she might decide to stop for other reasons, such as a non-smoking boyfriend who says that her breath smells. In this case a new form of friendship will have encouraged her to stop, just as it was originally friendship which encouraged her to start.

WHY START? DO INITIAL MOTIVATIONS MATTER?

The reasons for starting to use drugs is often thought of as resulting from 'hedonism' and the pursuit of pleasure, but this is rather unsatisfactory for a number of reasons, which will be explored in the following sections.

ACTIVITY 3.3
STARTING TO USE DRUGS

Spend 30 minutes on this activity.

In Chapter 2, Activity 2.7, you were asked to make notes while listening to the audio casette where Carl talks about the problems he has had to face as a result of taking drugs. Listen to this extract again and the extract of Peter talking about how he started using drugs. After listening make notes on why you think they started using drugs, what problems they had when starting and the way their drug taking went from experimentation to dependency. Compare these notes with the notes you made for Activity 2.7.

Comment

Carl seems to have decided to try drugs because they were around, part of the 'scene' in which he circulated, and some of his friends were using them. Friends passed the drugs on to him and despite the fact that he was violently ill during his first attempt, he was prepared to try again soon after when he was once again with drug using friends. Peter, too, started using drugs under similar circumstances together with his friends. At first they experimented from time to time, learning how to use the drugs, before moving into a stage of more frequent drug use.

The motives for starting to use drugs can perhaps be more usefully, even though very crudely, sub-divided into two categories: either to take part in various forms of social intercourse (e.g. the pub, the party); or to escape from social intercourse (e.g. oblivion drinking, distancing oneself from self and others). If this distinction holds good, then does it define for us the difference between 'drug use' and 'drug misuse'? Probably not. In their study of the careers of heroin users and the accounts which they gave of their experiences with heroin, Stimson and Oppenheimer (1982) identify two routes to heroin dependence. The first they describe as social accounts whereby a person first 'turned on' with friends, and the second they describe as psychological accounts where a person first 'turned on' alone. In the first case it was very much a question of people wanting to participate in an activity with friends. In the second case Stimson and Oppenheimer suggest that we are dealing with essentially lonely people whose initial experiences with heroin were described as personal, rather than a shared experience, and who referred to 'emotional difficulties, unhappiness or suicidal feelings' (ibid., p. 72–3). But if this second set of reasons sounds like a more 'pathological' initial motivation, which it undoubtedly was, these different initiations did not seem to determine the overall outcomes of heroin use. They did not find that one form of initiation into heroin use was more harmful than the other.

What seemed to be more important in determining the outcomes of heroin use were the subsequent social experiences in which drug use takes place. Stimson (1973) had earlier shown that heroin use was compatible with a wide variety of lifestyles, and that the stereotypical idea of the 'junkie' and a chaotic lifestyle was by no means typical and that many people who used heroin were able to sustain fairly ordinary commitments to their families and to employment.

Stimson suggested that heroin users could be classified according to four ideal-types: the 'stables'; the 'junkies'; the 'loners'; and the 'two-worlders'. The 'stables' led more or less normal lifestyles, eating and sleeping regularly, having little or nothing to do with other drug users and restricting themselves largely to drugs prescribed by medical practitioners and clinics as a result of their drug dependence. The 'junkies' were the opposite. They did not work, and supported themselves by stealing and hustling. They were heavily involved with other drug users, using illicit drugs from the black market, taking few health precautions such as using sterile needles, and with an unkempt and unconventional appearance. 'Loners' had little contact with other drug users and depended financially on social security benefits rather than stealing, and unlike the 'junkies' they tended to use their drugs alone rather than in the company of other users or in public places. 'Two-worlders' were somewhere between the 'stables' and the 'junkies', with high levels of criminal activity and high involvements with other drug users, although they also maintained involvements with the non-drug world and were typically in employment, taking few risks with dirty needles and syringes, eating and sleeping regularly, and were relatively conventional in appearance.

The differences between these groups of heroin users were fashioned largely by the extent to which they were involved in the local drug culture. Where people had cut themselves off from the drug culture, as with the 'stables' and 'loners', their drug use resulted in fewer cases of ill health and criminal convictions or institutionalization.

These findings have important implications for understanding drug use, because clearly the different outcomes of heroin use could not be a result of the pharmacological properties of the drug. Rather, we might say that the wider social contacts of these people mediated the pharmacological effects of heroin and helped to shape the different meanings which heroin use had for people.

ACTIVITY 3.4
'BECOMING A MARIHUANA USER'

Spend 25 minutes on this activity.

In his article, 'Becoming a marihuana user', Howard Becker has suggested that if someone is to become a 'successful' marijuana user, then there are a number of stages through which they must pass. You should now read this case study which has been reproduced in the Reader. As you study this article analyse its contents by writing a brief description of each of the milestones identified by Becker. When you have completed the article see if you can draw a schematic diagram which relates all the milestones together.

Comment

Essentially, what Becker is saying is that becoming a marijuana user is a learning process, and that the drug's effects are not immediately enjoyable, nor even recognizable. The three most important stages in this learning process are: (a) learning the technique of smoking; (b) learning to perceive the drug's effects; (c) learning to enjoy the effects.

Becker says that the novice user does not usually get 'high' on the first occasion that they use the drug, and that this is often because they do not smoke it properly. If the simple technique of inhaling the drug was not learnt then 'marijuana use was considered meaningless and did not continue'. Next, the novice user must learn to identify the effects of marijuana which, Becker suggests, are not always self-evident and sometimes involve only subtle alterations of consciousness. The novice user might only recognize a sense of dizziness, or a tingling sensation, which might not be connected with drug use. These connections must be learned, often from more experienced users. Finally, Becker suggests that the novice user must 'learn to enjoy the effects he has just learned to experience'.

Marijuana's pharmacological effects, as he describes them, are ambiguous. The altered perception of time, for example, might be experienced as quite frightening, if the users feel that they are losing control of their mental faculties. It is only through interaction with more experienced marijuana users that someone will learn, in effect, what 'pleasure' is and how the experiences produced by marijuana can be 'enjoyed'. Having reached this point, someone will have discovered the motivation to continue to use marijuana for pleasure.

BECKER'S MARIJUANA STUDY APPLIED TO OTHER DRUGS

Becker's work on marijuana use has been enormously influential in shaping understanding of initial drug user careers, although there are a number of criticisms which can be made about his approach. For example, it tends to neglect the pharmacological basis of drug induced experiences. While people can experience 'placebo' effects from drugs, whereby they imagine that the drug has produced certain desired effects (whether getting 'high' or curing a headache) which are only the result of the user's expectations, drugs do nevertheless possess real and definable pharmacological properties. Experiences from marijuana use, for example, are different from those of drinking alcohol, which are in turn quite different from taking an aspirin. Moreover, the experiences of marijuana users do not always conform to those described by Becker, in that some people will say that they did not need to pass through a learning stage and that the drug had an immediate and powerful effect on them (Pearson & Twohig, 1976).

Even so, it will be helpful to pause at this point and think through the possible implications of Becker's study of marijuana use for other kinds of drug use. In particular, how does his suggestion that it is first necessary to learn how to enjoy the effects of a drug before pleasure-seeking becomes a meaningful motivation for drug use related to other pharmacological agents?

People will be first introduced to most drugs through friends, and although the pursuit of pleasure might form part of this friendship network, the initial reasons for trying a drug might well have more to do with sharing in an activity with friends. The pursuit of pleasure will have even less relevance in relation to drugs such as medically prescribed tranquillizers. Here the initial motive might be to escape from burdensome worries, although a person will typically wish to escape from worries not because of 'hedonism', but in order to be able to carry out a variety of practical tasks (domestic duties, employment responsibilities) more successfully. It is possible that someone might subsequently discover that the use of tranquillizers is pleasurable, but that will not be the initial reason for consulting the doctor. The pleasure-seeking model for starting to use drugs also fails to acknowledge that when someone first tries a drug it will often make them feel ill. Whether we think of the unpleasant dizzying effect of the first 'drag' on a cigarette as a child, the sickness and hangover of the first experience of being drunk, or the nausea which often accompanies the first time that a person experiments with heroin, pleasure-seeking can hardly be described as the most obvious motivation.

Becker's model seems quite a good way to describe the initial experiences with a variety of drugs. Smoking cigarettes 'successfully' (that is, in order to find them pleasurable) will require the novice smoker to master the initially unpleasant effects, in such a way as to experience the dizziness as a pleasurable sensation.

Novice drinkers must also learn how to control their intake (i.e. to learn the technique of alcohol consumption) if they are to gain any pleasure from drinking. Even so, some people will never learn to experience the effects of either alcohol or tobacco as pleasurable (reminding us once again that pleasure is not inherent in the pharmacology) or they will find that their effects conflict with other pursuits which are valued more highly. Some people do not like to drink alcohol even in small quantities, for example, because they prefer to keep a 'clear head' or because they fear the loss of self-control, whereas other people like alcohol because it helps them to relax and feel more at ease with themselves and in company. In general, for someone to continue any form of drug use, this will have to be successfully integrated within a satisfying social context, otherwise drug use will have no meaning for them.

3.4 DIFFERENT LEVELS OF DRUG INVOLVEMENT

In the preceding section the concept of a drug user's 'career' was introduced, and now a simple 'career model' for drug involvements will be outlined and applied to a variety of different drugs. This model will then be followed through in some detail in relation to heroin use. The approach will be both to indicate something specifically about heroin and how people become involved with the drug, while still pointing to similarities in user careers between otherwise dissimilar drugs.

A DECISION-MAKING CAREER MODEL

A very simple model of a drug-user career has already been described which involved three stages: initiation into drug use; the continuation of drug use; and the cessation of drug use. An individual's movement between these different stages is understood within such a 'career model' as involving a variety of decision-making processes, and a close examination of these decisions and how they are arrived at can help to clarify how and why people make different drug choices. A decision-making approach to drug use and drug misuse is therefore quite different from the 'pathological' model, which sees heroin use as a consequence of certain people with 'addictive personalities' falling prey to the addictive pharmacological properties of the drug

(Bennett, 1986). 'Career' models and 'decision-making' models, by contrast, lay greater emphasis on rational choices in the development of drug careers and this perspective has enormous practical importance for preventive health and health education where the aim is to encourage people to make more sensible drug choices.

Different authors at different times have suggested variations to the career model. In her book *Women on Heroin,* for example, Marsha Rosenbaum reviewed a variety of different approaches to the 'careers' or 'life histories' of heroin users, and suggested that they shared a number of common characteristics which she grouped under five headings:

1 An initial stage when people explore drug use lifestyles

2 A 'becoming' stage when regular visits into drug user life are made as an apprentice

3 A 'maintaining' phase when opiates are used regularly and the individual takes on a drug user social identity and commitment

4 An 'on again, off again' stage when users slowly find drug use alternately functional and dysfunctional (this is usually accompanied by regular stays in jail and treatment centres)

5 A conversation phase when the drug user intends to become clean permanently (Rosenbaum, 1981, pp. 15–16).

What I intend to propose here is a simple four-phase model which does no more than describe the different levels of involvement which a person might have with a drug, as their drug-using career develops:

1   The non-use
2   The initial offer and experimentation
3(a) Occasional use on a recreational basis
3(b) The 'grey area' of transitional use
4   Dependency.

Let us first consider in broad outline how this model might apply to someone's involvement with heroin. Each step between these different stages represents a vital movement in a heroin user's career. So, the non-user having been offered the drug will either accept or reject it. If the offer is accepted and the person tries it on an 'experimental' basis, they might either discontinue their experimentation quite quickly because they do not enjoy the experience, or they might embark on a more prolonged period of experimentation. At this point they might begin a pattern of recreational use on a very occasional basis, and continue this pattern of recreational use over a long period of time without becoming dependent. Heroin is, of course, a highly addictive drug. Nevertheless, non-compulsive patterns of opiate use have been identified in both Britain and North America, although these are forms of drug use which can quickly run out of control if strict safeguards are not adhered to (Zinberg, 1984; Blackwell, 1984; Pearson, 1987). Indeed, if someone begins to use heroin on more than a very infrequent basis, then they enter upon what may be called the 'grey area' of transitional use. In this phase it is not clear whether or not they are becoming dependent. It is a phase of heroin use where the person's status of involvement with the drug is open to misinterpretation which is why I call it the 'grey area'. And finally, if this pattern of transitional use continues for any length of time the heroin user will suffer an imperceptible drift into dependency.

Each of these phases can be thought of as different statuses of heroin involvement, and the passage between them as transition points. For the purposes of health education and service provision, they imply different audiences, with vastly different needs. The transition points might also be regarded as crucial targets for health education, where this aims to limit a person's involvement with drugs and to arrest their involvement at a particular point. Finally, each status will imply different possible exit routes towards abstinence. Indeed, one important difference between this model and those previously mentioned is that it does not imply that a person needs to pass through all the various stages of a drug-using career before moving to the abstinence phase: people can, and do, keep their drug use at lower levels of involvement and then subsequently stop.

This model was originally developed in the context of research on heroin use in the North of England (Pearson et al., 1986). Nevertheless, it has a wider range of applications which can help to show up some common features of different kinds of drug use careers. How does this model relate, for example, to alcohol, tobacco, cannabis and tranquillizers? For each of these drugs it is possible to identify the same statuses of involvement and transition points: the non-user; the initial offer and experimentation; occasional use; and habitual use.

Nevertheless, different social meanings will be attached to each status for different drugs. In the case of tranquillizers, for example, the 'initial offer' will have come from a medical practitioner and 'experimentation' will usually involve a testing out of whether the doctor's prescription helps to ease the problem about which he or she was consulted. Whereas in the case of cannabis, this will more typically involve sharing in an activity among friends, or simple curiosity.

There will also be various timescales by which people move between different statuses of drug involvement. In the case of tobacco, for example, once a person has established a pattern of occasional use they will often move very quickly to a pattern of dependent, habitual use. Whereas a pattern of occasional alcohol use, or 'social drinking', may commonly remain stable for many years or even a whole lifetime; and if a pattern of alcohol dependency is to develop, then this will take a long period of time. In a similar way, the vast bulk of people who smoke cannabis will use it only on an occasional, recreational basis.

Finally, it is important to note that these different patterns of response will be shaped not only by the pharmacological properties of different drugs, together with individual and cultural preferences, but also questions of drug availability and distribution. Most people will have been exposed to alcohol and tobacco at some point in their lives, for example, whereas only a tiny minority of the overall population will ever have access to heroin.

One consequence of different patterns of drug involvement is that at any point in time within a drug-using population, people will be distributed differently between the various statuses of involvement in relation to different drugs. A diagrammatic representation of user-profiles is presented in the figure below, which distinguishes between the statuses of non-user, experimentation, occasional user and habitual user in relation to alcohol, tobacco, cannabis, tranquillizers and heroin. This figure can only show the approximate similarities and peculiarities of various forms of drug use and drug misuse.

APPROXIMATE USER–PROFILES OF FIVE DIFFERENT DRUGS, ACCORDING TO STATUS OF INVOLVEMENT

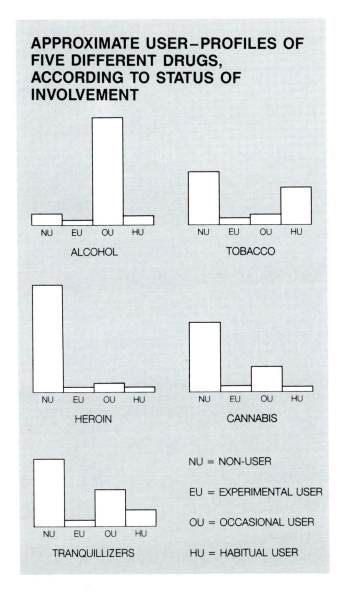

NU = NON-USER

EU = EXPERIMENTAL USER

OU = OCCASIONAL USER

HU = HABITUAL USER

HEROIN USER CAREERS: MYTHS AND MEANINGS

We now need to turn to a detailed consideration of a heroin user's career. Heroin is a drug surrounded by considerable notoriety and an extensive mythology, as if it were totally different from any other drug. One aim of this discussion is to unravel some of this mythology. It is commonly believed, for example, that people who try heroin always become dependent. It is important to recognize at the outset, therefore, that people's encounters with heroin can sometimes have very different outcomes.

Cheryl, Wayne and Wendy are three friends in their early twenties who have all used heroin. Cheryl and Wayne are sister and brother, and Wendy is Wayne's girlfriend. When Cheryl first tried heroin with a friend, she found it highly enjoyable and quickly developed what she called a 'greedy' habit. She supported this habit largely through shoplifting for more than two years, mixing almost entirely in the company of other heroin users, until she was eventually caught and placed in custody. She now receives a prescription for methadone from a local psychiatric clinic.

Wayne, on the other hand, was someone who had used heroin and did not like it. He was with his sister at a party where the drug was being used, he was curious about it and tried it. The drug made him violently ill, and he had never been tempted to try it since. 'That was the first and last', said Wayne, 'I just thought, "Scrub that". You know what I mean? No chance.'

Wendy first encountered heroin when she was offered it by a boyfriend. At first she always refused it because she was frightened, but then one day she accepted the offer and began to use it regularly. However, although she used it daily for about six months she says that she 'wasn't that bothered' about it. 'I liked the buzz', she said, but then after six months she stopped. This was because she discovered that, unlike Cheryl, she was always afraid that she might get caught shoplifting, and decided that her liberty was more important than heroin. Then she met Wayne, who had disliked heroin so much, and she has never been tempted to use it since then.

We can see, in the radically different experiences of these three friends, that in their encounters with heroin, and as people move from one status to another, conscious choices will sometimes become apparent to the individual. But equally, a person can move imperceptibly from one status to another without any conscious decision making. This is perhaps especially the case in the patterns of transitional use which take a person from the status of occasional use to compulsive use and dependency. At this fateful transition point it is not uncommon for someone dependent on heroin to say that they were taken by surprise when they first experienced withdrawal symptoms, sometimes to the extent that they did not even identify what these symptoms were.

The decisions which people make at different transition points may be influenced by a variety of factors, particularly questions of friendship. The circumstances of the initial offer, for example, are that heroin will be invariably first offered to someone within a friendship network. It is now a basis of firm agreement by researchers both in North America and Britain that the stereotype of the 'pusher' hanging around school playgrounds, luring young people into addiction with 'free samples' is a myth and most unhelpful for the purposes of health education, etc. (Preble & Casey (Reader); Moore, 1977; Bennett & Wright, 1986; Pearson et al., 1986; Pearson, 1987).

It is vitally important, for health education purposes, to correct this myth, because if one of the aims of health education is to encourage people to 'say no' to drugs, then they must first know what it is that they will be required to say no to: the gift of a friend, and not the wiles of a stranger and 'pusher'. The friendship will, of course, make the drug offer more likely to be accepted. This is all the more reason to situate the question of friendship very firmly in our understanding of drug-using careers, as well as in prevention programmes which attempt to limit drug involvements, rather than to try to frighten people with myths and stereotypes.

Another unhelpful myth is that heroin is instantly addictive. There is, in fact, nothing inevitable about the passage from one status to another in the career of a heroin user. Some people slide rapidly into habitual use and dependency, following a pattern of progressive decline and increasing drug consumption. But other people can, and do, arrest their involvement at different

points within this hierarchy of statuses. Some people discontinue their heroin use after a brief flirtation with the drug, for example, whereas others maintain stable patterns of occasional use over long periods of time. According to some authorities the very idea of non-addictive heroin use is an anathema; a view summed up in the title of a book by Smith and Gay (1972), It's so good, don't even try it once. However, extensive research in North America by Norman Zinberg and his colleagues has established that non-compulsive opiate use is not only a possibility if certain rules on the frequency of use are strictly adhered to, such as only using ther drug very occasionally and never on consecutive days, but that patterns of occasional heroin use are much more commonly practised than habitual daily use patterns (Zinberg, 1984).

Finally, exit routes will also vary considerably within this career model of heroin use. Different motivations trigger them, different methods are used to come off heroin, and different timescales are involved. Changes in friendship – a new boyfriend/girlfriend – will sometimes be the stimulus. The threat of imprisonment when someone has been arrested for a drug-related offence might be the motivating trigger. Others simply become tired of the heroin lifestyle, where for the dependent user the drug becomes an all-consuming preoccupation. For other people, however, this preoccupation is itself a major reason for continuing to use the drug because the way in which sufficient money and quantities of good quality heroin are obtained provides a structured daily routine and lends sense and meaning to life.

In moving towards abstinence some people try to make a clean break, while others try to withdraw slowly in stages by gradually reducing their intake. Some try to do it with professional assistance, whereas others do it on their own and see this as important if their abstinence is to be 'real'. A crucial distinction must be made between 'coming off', which for many heroin users is a relatively effortless experience akin to a bad dose of influenza, as against 'staying off' which is repeatedly said by heroin users themselves to be much more difficult.

One of the most unhelpful myths associated with heroin use concerns the notion of 'cold turkey' withdrawal symptoms. These are often described as always involving a horrifying experience far beyond the normal extremities of human pain. This is not the experience of a great many heroin users, however, and a new consensus is beginning to form around this question. This stresses that 'coming off' can be achieved without having to pass through the 'gates of hell' and offers the heroin user thinking about 'coming off' a much more positive and realistic picture of withdrawal. It once more raises the question of choice in the drug-user career. It is equally agreed, however, that once detoxification is accomplished – in a matter of ten days or so – then the real challenge is how to restructure one's life without drugs and to 'stay off' successfully.

This simple model could undoubtedly be refined, and it will be influenced by important considerations such as whether a person smokes or injects heroin. Indeed, the decision whether to cross the 'injection barrier' might be considered a vital transition point itself. This might also influence exit routes, so that someone who injects might first move onto smoking heroin for a time in order to overcome the commonly reported 'needle fixation', before attempting to come off the drug completely. Nevertheless, the model can serve usefully as a framework for thinking about different levels of drug involvement and how to target different audiences for the purposes of treatment services, counselling, health education etc. The different targets of 'non-user', 'experimental user' and 'confirmed user' also have important implications for law enforcement strategies and policing directed towards the heroin problem (Moore, 1977).

ACTIVITY 3.5
FROM 'ESCAPIST' TO
'RATIONAL ACTOR'

Spend 25 minutes on this activity.

You should now read the excerpt from 'Taking Care of Business' by Preble and Casey, in the Reader. This is a study of the life of street drug users in New York. As you read the article make a note of those points where the authors' account conflicts with what you think might be the common stereotype of heroin dependency.

Comment

What Preble and Casey have to say confirms a number of points in the preceding discussion of a heroin user's career. For example, that heroin will be passed onto novice users among friends and that the notion of the 'pusher' who entraps people in heroin dependency is unhelpful. Another interesting point is that it was not 'inadequate' young people who were most likely to become involved with heroin, but rather those who were more likely to be opinion leaders and gang leaders in their neighbourhood. Then, there is the question of how heroin use could come to be associated with high status within a friendship network, something which has been found in other North American research (Feldman, 1968).

However, perhaps the most surprising way in which Preble and Casey depart from the stereotype of heroin use is the way in which they describe this not as a 'passive' retreat from life, but rather an extremely active and exacting lifestyle. This is an important recognition which can help us to understand why heroin users so often say that 'staying off' is much more difficult than withstanding the physical withdrawal symptoms of 'coming off'. Heroin use embraces a whole way of life, and in attempting to 'stay off' and remain abstinent it is necessary for the ex-user to substitute a new set of daily routines in place of the hectic daily 'hustle' required to sustain a heroin habit. Some examples of how heroin users describe these difficulties, and try to come to terms with them, can be found in this article.

Throughout this chapter, stress has been placed on the importance of the social contexts of drug use and misuse, both in terms of what encourages people to use a drug in the first place, and also the obstacles that will be encountered when someone tries to stop using a drug. This sets the scene for the discussion in the next chapter on the control of drugs.

REFERENCES

Bennett, T. (1986) 'A Decision-Making Approach to Opioid Addiction', in D.B. Cornish & R.V. Clarke (eds.), *The Reasoning Criminal: Rational choice perspectives on offending*

Bennett, T. & Wright, R. (1986) 'The Drug-Taking Careers of Opioid Users', *Howard Journal of Criminal Justice*, Vol 25, No 1

Berridge, V. & Edwards, G. (1981) *Opium and the People*, Allen Lane

Blackwell, J.S. (1984) 'Drifting, Controlling and Overcoming: Opiate Users Who Avoid Becoming Chronically Dependent', *Journal of Drug Issues*, Vol 13, No 2

Feldman, H.W. (1968) 'Ideological Supports to Becoming and Remaining a Heroin Addict', *Journal of Health and Social Behaviour*, Vol 9

Hughes, P.H. *et al.* (1972) 'The Natural History of a Heroin Epidemic', *American Journal of Public Health*, Vol 62, No 7

Lacey, R. & Woodward, S. (1985) *That's Life! Survey on Tranquillisers*, BBC/MIND

McConville, B. (1983) *Women Under the Influence: Alcohol and its impact*, Virago

Malyon, T. (1985) 'Love Seeds and Cash Crop: The Cannabis Commodity Market', in A. Henman *et al.*, *Big Deal: The Politics of the Illicit Drugs Business*, Pluto

Mass Observation (1943) *The Pub and the People*, Gollancz

Moore, M.H. (1977) *Buy and Bust: The Effective Regulation of an Illicit Market in Heroin*, Lexington, Mass., D.C. Heath

Parker, H.J., Bakx, K., & Newcombe, R. (1986) *Drug Misuse in Wirral: A Study of Eighteen Hundred Problem Drug Users*, Liverpool: University of Liverpool

Pearson, G. (1987) *The New Heroin Users: Voices from the Street*, Blackwell

Pearson, G., & Twohig, J. (1976) 'Ethnography Through the Looking Glass: The Case of Howard Becker', in S. Hall & T. Jefferson (eds.) *Resistance Through Rituals*, Hutchinson

Pearson, G., Gilman, M. & McIver, S. (1986) *Young People and Heroin: An Examination of Heroin Use in the North of England*, Health Education Council and Gower

Plant, M.A., Peck, D.F., & Samuel, E. (1985) *Alcohol, Drugs and School-Leavers*, Tavistock

Rosenbaum, M. (1981) *Women on Heroin*, Rutgers UP

Smith, D.E. & Gay, G.R. (eds.) (1972) *It's So Good, Don't Even Try it Once*, Prentice-Hall

Stimson, G.V. (1973) *Heroin and Behaviour*, Irish UP

Stimson, G.V. & Oppenheimer, E. (1982) *Heroin Addiction*, Tavistock

Zinberg, N.E. (1984) *Drug, Set and Setting: The Basis for Controlled Intoxicant Use*, Yale UP

4 THE CONTROL OF DRUGS

4.1 INTRODUCTION

In this chapter you will be introduced to some key issues in the control of legal and illegal drugs. The first sections look at the issues historically, contrasting the emergence of increasingly punitive control upon opiate drugs (such as heroin – made from opium), with the relatively free and increasingly large markets in alcohol and tobacco. The chapter then moves on to look at British policy against 'illegal' drugs in the post-war period, focussing upon drug controls in the 1980s. The implications of control strategies for those who work with users are discussed in the final section.

4.2 EXAMPLES FROM HISTORY

OPIUM: FROM PROFITS TO PENALTIES

The history of drug controls is a long one which it might repay many modern policy makers to study. The development of the Far Eastern trade in opium, its subsequent suppression and accompanying international agreements, offers a particularly interesting case study.

The emergence of *The Opium Question* in the nineteenth century had its roots firmly planted in British trade relations with China. From around the end of the eighteenth century the British East India Company was engaged in the export of opium to China in exchange for tea. British trade policy was aimed at expanding this market, a prospect not welcomed by the Chinese. At least initially, this was not necessarily only for moral or health reasons but also because of concern that excessive expenditure of silver on opium was upsetting the country's balance of trade (Teff, 1973). Attempts by China to end the nature of this trade led to two periods of conflict known as the Opium Wars, taking place between 1839–42 and 1857–8. For Britain the purpose of the wars was not merely to maintain its opium trade but also to open up the Chinese market to other western goods. China was eventually defeated and obliged to continue to accept 'free trade', including importation of opium (Inglis, 1975 and 1976).

From around the 1840s onward, a growing body of influential opinion in Britain began to criticize the opium trade as morally indefensible. Elements of concern about China being the unwilling recipient of opium and about the possible harmful effects of use of the drug began to make their mark. Debates in Parliament slowly but surely drew more support to the anti-opium lobby and campaigning organizations such as the Society for the Suppression of the Opium Trade were established (in 1874).

THE EGYPTIAN EXAMPLE: A QUITE MODERN CONTROL DILEMMA

Concern about opium and its use and commercial trade was not limited to China and Britain. Other nations were also inventing drug control measures during the late nineteenth century. Egypt, for example, then a British Protectorate, was concerned with the effect of both hashish and opium on its labour force. A variety of efforts had been made to control by imposing a heavy duty or by prohibition, with severe penalties for possession.

Interestingly, the preferred control strategy of the senior police official with responsibility for drugs control in Egypt offers an early parallel to some arguments put forward in the 1960s for a more liberal attitude to be taken towards use of cannabis (hashish), with a more punitive line being taken towards use (and especially supply) of opiates. This idea (as put forward to the Egyptian government by Thomas Russell in the 1920s) was no more acceptable to authorities then than it proved to be in the 1960s (Wootton Report 1968).

Russell's tasks as Director of Egypt's Central Narcotics Bureau remain familiar ones for law enforcement and control today:

● improving the customs service

● developing reliable informants (which could prove to be a very expensive business)

● detecting cleverly concealed consignments

● trying to trace the chain of operation upwards to the organizers of the smuggling and distribution.

The Egyptian authorities found that, if police action against one drug proved to be successful, then the resultant scarcity of certain drugs simply pushed up prices and shifted demand to other drugs – sometimes with serious consequences. When opium and hashish became scarce, users turned instead to a mixture of tobacco and henbane – impossible to deal with effectively by police measures, as tobacco was too well established to ban, and henbane (another plant drug) grew wild (Inglis, 1975, p. 173).

OPERATION INTERCEPT

We can compare the historical Egyptian drug control problem with a more recent one in the USA. In 1969 the US government mounted a major campaign, called Operation Intercept, against marijuana importation

across the US–Mexican border. A study of this initiative found that: 'During the summer of 1969 the government-enforced marijuana shortage was a key factor underlying the widespread use of illicit drugs other than marijuana. Essentially this suggests that . . . one way in which the "softer to harder" [drug use] formulation becomes a reality for the individual drug user is grounded in the limited availability of the "softer" drug' (Gooberman, 1974, p. 187).

No one wants to be too pessimistic about the possibility of controlling drug supply, demand and distribution. However, it must be recognized that well-intentioned policies sometimes have disastrous unintended consequences.

4.3   CONTRASTS BETWEEN ALCOHOL AND TOBACCO AND THE ILLEGAL DRUGS

In recent years as more concern has been expressed by government, the media and the general public about illegal drugs, some have argued that the more serious health problems related to alcohol and tobacco consumption have been overlooked or not taken seriously enough; that it is at these substances that serious control measures should be directed.

A recent report on *Comparative mortality from drugs of addiction*, published by the British Medical Association and Action on Alcohol Abuse (1986, p. 1), notes for example, that:

'Deaths caused directly by illicit drugs (235 in 1984) are but a fraction of deaths caused by tobacco (100 000 a year) or alcohol (5000–8000) . . . Tobacco and alcohol related diseases are susceptible to prevention yet the government does little. Illicit drugs, by definition do not benefit the government, but taxes on alcohol raise revenue of £6000 million a year, and tobacco over £4000 million. Both are produced in the UK by large multi-national companies.'

On health grounds alone, there would seem to be a case to be made for some form of restriction or control on consumption of tobacco and alcohol, yet the modern direction of control flows in a different direction, aimed particularly at opiates and the negative legal and health consequences of their use. Recent government anti-heroin campaigns have tried to convey a certain image of heroin users and the dangers they face. It is with some irony, then, that we can find a physician of the seventeenth century warning of tobacco that it is 'not safe for youth; it shorteneth life; it breedeth many diseases; it breedeth melancholy; it hurteth the mind; it is ill for the smoker's issue' (quoted in Bewley, 1969, p. 7).

Present-day controls over licensing hours for the sale of alcohol originate largely in provisions of the Defence of the Realm (Amendment) Act of 1915. Temperance and state interests found some common ground here as restrictions over the production and sale of alcohol came into force as a contribution to the maintenance of national efficiency and production during wartime.

Today, controls over alcohol are administered formally and informally in myriad ways:

● by the passage of laws (for example, liberalizing the Scottish laws, tightening up others)

● by the police and judiciary

● by health education messages

● by price (a major determinant of this being government taxation)

● and by family and friends.

ACTIVITY 4.1
THE LEGAL STATUS OF ALCOHOL AND TOBACCO

Spend about 15 minutes on this activity.

Why do you think alcohol and tobacco have escaped legislation to ban their use? Note down three reasons.

Comment

You may have noted some of the reasons given below:

● Governments earn large amounts of revenue from taxes levied on alcohol and tobacco.

● Powerful interests – breweries, distilleries, tobacco companies, and sometimes governments themselves – promote and protect the market (Taylor, 1984).

● The industries employ hundreds of thousands of people in production, distribution, retail trade (and, indirectly, in advertising and selling).

● Many more people use tobacco and alcohol than use illegal drugs. Legislation against use would be extremely unpopular and probably unenforceable.

● Most people believe, rightly or wrongly, that alcohol and tobacco are less dangerous than illegal drugs, this belief legitimizes the different legal statuses of the legal and illegal drugs.

Dorn ('Drink and Political Economy' in the Reader) argues that alcohol and tobacco industries are significant parts of the broader economy, and that, in Britain, the state has never attempted to redress overall production of alcohol or tobacco; controls have been restricted to the sphere of the consumption. Now read this paper.

Dorn notes the importance of the drinks industry as a leading section of UK capital. It contributes to:

● employment, particularly in distribution and retail sectors

● government income through taxation and the balance of trade.

4.4 SOCIAL REACTIONS TO USERS OF OPIATES AND OTHER DRUGS

Social anxiety about drug use may sometimes be understood as alarm about, or denigration of, those who are using the drugs.

RACE, LABOUR MARKET AND DRUGS CONTROL

The United States has played a major role in the formulation of international regulations and controls over opiates and other drugs. However, the historical origins of drug controls within the United States have little to do with international diplomacy and economic interests abroad; US domestic drug laws have rather more to do with responses to a changing labour market at home.

In the late 1860s and 1870s a wave of poor Chinese immigrants began to arrive in California. In a booming economy they easily found work in railroad construction, farming, mining, or the newly developing manufacturing industries of San Francisco. As Helmer and Vietorisz observe, whatever the actual amount of opium use among the Chinese population in the boom years, there certainly seems to be no public record of concern about it, indeed 'labour contractors themselves offered an allowance of half a pound of opium per month as a bonus above wages to attract Chinese labourers' (Helmer and Vietorisz, 1974, p. 4).

As long as there remained a high demand for labour then the immigant Chinese were welcome, but as soon as a depression struck and wages dropped, a strong anti-Chinese backlash followed. With the sharp decline in economic growth, the Chinese workers formed a large pool of cheap surplus labour which could be attractive to farming, mining and rail interests – but very threatening to a white working class seeking work and preferential wages. Among many other issues, the use of opium became a potent symbol to fuel anti-Chinese sentiments:

'It was part of the hostile stereotype of the Chinese which appeared in popular circulation to justify and legitimise the whole working class ideology of the time. Not until the depression struck was any official notice taken of the opium dens, and even then it was never suggested that the use of the drug was harmful *per se*.

It was its character as a Chinese habit, not as a narcotic, which warranted the earliest legislation against opium in the country, enacted by the San Francisco municipal authority in 1875' (ibid., pp. 5–6).

Similar connections between American drug controls, and labour market conditions and racism, have been documented in relation to marijuana (and its use by Mexican labourers) and in relation to cocaine (and anti-black movements in the South). See Helmer (1975).

There are also issues in relation to drugs control and race in Britain that you might like to consider. There are several ways in which issues around race and issues around drugs overlap. The most obvious issue is the use of cannabis by Rastafarians as a sacrament in the context of particular religious beliefs, and the question of whether police action against Rastafarians should be regarded as racist interference or as legitimate crime control. This, however, is a clear case of a section of an ethnic group having a particular relationship to an illegal drug. In many ethnic groups the use of illegal drugs (especially heroin) is probably less common than amongst the white population, and some particular religious groups (e.g. Muslims) explicitly forbid intoxication with any drug, including alcohol.

POST WAR SOCIAL REACTIONS TO YOUTHFUL USE OF DRUGS

Within Britain, drugs other than alcohol and tobacco have been a focus for public concern and government action at several times in the post-war period.

During the middle and late 1960s there were concerns about amphetamines, cannabis, and heroin; then during the 1970s the market in illegal drugs expanded further, and solvent sniffing became more common and perceived as a form of drug use; finally in the early to mid 1980s rapidly increasing importation, distribution and use of heroin (mainly for smoking rather than injection) led to new initiatives at the levels of government policy, local authority services and community action.

Of course it was heroin that became and has since remained the focus of public policy. Up until the early 1960s, the heroin problem was thought to be contained, there being only a few hundred users of the drug, nearly all of whom got their supplies quite legally from medical practitioners. The Brain Report of 1961 surveyed the situation up to that time and concluded that no change was needed in the policy of supply. By the mid 1960s, however, it had become clear that a 'grey market' had

developed in the sale of heroin that had been obtained from doctors, and that new users were being recruited into the injection scene. The Brain Committee reconvened in 1965 and recommended changes which led to the setting up of specialist Drug Dependency Units ('drug clinics') in 1968.

ACTIVITY 4.2
POST-WAR POLICIES ON HEROIN

Spend about 40 minutes on this activity.

For a description of the British response to heroin use and a discussion of the development of law enforcement and treatment measures now read the Reader article, 'British Drug Policies in the 1980s', by Gerry Stimson. As you do so note down the main policy assumptions and trends in:

(a) The mid/late 60s

(b) The 70s

(c) The 80s

Comment

(a) The 'British System' in relation to heroin control in the 1960s was both medical and penal: users were treated for an 'illness' if accepted by medical staff as being addicted to heroin or similar drugs, but were open to prosecution if found in possession of opiate (or other illegal drugs) not prescribed by a doctor.

(b) Therapeutic 'contracts' were made with users as the basis for their treatment and receipt of prescribed drugs.

(c) NHS Drug Dependency Units (clinics) remained important well into the 1980s, but were joined by non-statutory agencies (rehabilitation houses, street agencies) and non-specialist agencies. The number of seizures and prosecutions increased. Drug enforcement came to the fore as part of the 'law and order' politics of the 1980s.

4.5 OVERVIEW OF BRITISH DRUG CONTROL IN THE 1980s

You may want to remind yourself of the current law on scheduling, classification and penalties. If you do, now read the ISDD Information Service Briefing paper on the Misuse Of Drugs Act reproduced in the Reader.

ACTIVITY 4.3
'TACKLING DRUG MISUSE'

Spend about 20 minutes on this activity.

The 1986 policy document produced by the government; 'Tackling Drug Misuse' summarizes their approach as follows:

● reducing supplies from abroad

● making enforcement even more effective

● strengthening deterrence and tightening domestic controls

● developing prevention

● improving treatment and rehabilitation.

The strategy is reprinted in an edited version of 'Tackling Drug Misuse' (section 2). Enforcement policies are discussed in section 4, and controls and deterrence in section 5. *Please note:* The strategy is updated periodically, to take account of new initiatives. At the time of going to press there have been increases in customs staffing and resources. Changes currently seem to be directed at increasing resources, rather than at changing policy significantly.

Now read the edited extracts in the Reader and note the different strategies suggested to reduce drug use.

Comment

You will have noted the increasing emphasis on deterrence in Chapter 4, and on penalties in Chapter 5. Did you note the powers of the Court to confiscate from drug traffickers all the property that they possess that they cannot show was obtained without the aid of the financial proceeds of possible acts of drug supply?

Bear in mind that penalties for confiscation of assets apply only in the case of trafficking in and supply of drugs, and can be imposed in addition to fines and prison sentences (up to life imprisonment in the case of trafficking in drugs such as heroin). Possession of controlled drugs (i.e. for personal use) is also illegal, of course, but the penalties are lower. You may need to look back at Tables 2 and 3 in the ISDD Information Service Briefing, for information on the maximum penalties that can be imposed in a magistrate's court ('summary') and before a judge after jury trial ('indictment').

HEAVIER PENALTIES FOR SUPPLIERS: WHAT IS THEIR EFFECTIVENESS?

Penalties for drug dealing have been increased three times in the post-war period in Britain, yet supply of heroin, in particular, has increased markedly. There are a number of views that can help to explain this. In the following activity we ask you to think about a range of views. The activity is in two parts. In the first we want you to listen to, and read through, a range of views, and in the second part, to make some notes about your own views.

ACTIVITY 4.4(a)
VIEWS ON PENALTIES FOR TRAFFICKING AND SUPPLY

(Activity 3a on audio)

This should take you about 20 minutes.

Two short interviews are provided for you on audiotape.

'A' is a street agency worker

'B' is a probation officer

Now play the tape and listen to these interviews. While you are doing so make brief notes on the views expressed.

Comment

'A' noted that penalty enforcement was catching the small, instead of the big, 'fish', and so making it more difficult to help the users.

'B' also mentioned this, commenting that harsh penalties do not seem to be a deterrent to 'the lads at the top' who will 'have a go if they think they can get away with it'.

Other perspectives that can be brought to bear are:

● Penalties have yet to bite because they are not yet high enough. This view has been influential in the United States, where legislation drafted in 1986 attracted amendments to increase to death the maximum penalty for trafficking.

● Penalties have deterred suppliers (and/or possessors) and have slowed down the growth of the problem: without these penalties, the problem would be worse than it is today.

● Nothing would make much difference, because
a) the trade is simply a response to demand for drugs, this demand being stimulated by unemployment, lack of parental discipline, lack of alternative pleasures . . .

b) and/or the trade has deep economic roots and cannot be eradicated, especially in a recession when there is a dearth of legitimate and profitable small business opportunities . . .

c) and/or the source of the problem does not lie with the jurisdiction of the British courts, but in the countries from which opium is cultivated, converted to heroin and pressed upon our shores.

The available evidence does not allow us to say with certainty that any of the above views is correct.

Perhaps you yourself do subscribe to one or two of the viewpoints above – or perhaps you find it easier to say which ones you disagree with!

ACTIVITY 4.4(b)
YOUR VIEWS ON PENALTIES FOR TRAFFICKING AND SUPPLY

Allow about 30 minutes for this activity.

Write down, on a couple of sheets of paper:

● some notes about all the evidence you can think of (or collect) to support a particular view (or to counter other views), and

● some notes about the ways in which you would need to present and argue your evidence when in front of one of the following audiences: Magistrates Association; young people in a youth club; your professional colleagues; your family or friends.

Comment

Doing this activity may have prompted you to find out more, and think more deeply about, different views, and how you can work with them.

THE INTERNATIONAL DIMENSION: TACKLING THE PROBLEM AT SOURCE

One of the reactions that we may have, when faced with what seems a very complex and possibly insurmountable problem at home, is to say, 'can't we stop the problem at source?' What most people mean by this is stopping drugs coming into the country. This is indeed part of government policy, as you saw when reading the 'Tackling Drug Misuse' extracts. Some experts, however, are sceptical about the success of this approach. Stimson argues that policy measures need to be extended to the Third World countries where drugs are produced. You may now wish to read this paper which is reproduced in the Reader (Stimson, 'Can a War on Drugs Succeed?').

A résumé of the present government's ideas about international action can be found in the current (1987) complete version of the Home Office strategy paper. The main strategy involves working as part of the UN Commission on Narcotic Drugs to co-operate with producer and transit countries by:

● law enforcement (preventing people from growing illicit crops)

● crop eradication (wiping out crops which are being grown unlawfully)

● crop substitution/rural development (encouraging the growing of new crops in place of illicit crops)

● providing the necessary infrastructure so that there will be no incentive to revert to illicit crops.

It is conceded, however, that these strategies present considerable problems, largely related to cost and manpower. One major problem, not discussed in the Home Office document, is the pressure for quick results. UN and US agencies are constrained by their objective of short-term results. This binds them to relatively rapid, top-down methods of development, featuring opportunistic alliances with powerful local interest groups and middle-to-large size landlords (main recipients of the gains of the Green Revolution), and reliance on levels of technology that may not be maintainable in the longer term. These features limit the scope for wide support and durability of development. Such reservations have a familiar ring to them, for they are part of the well known critique of development programmes. Development agencies and their staff are well aware of these historic problems; they act as they do, not because they are stupid or ill-intentioned, but because of the pressures upon them from their Western sponsors for quick results.

Some of this pressure comes from Britain, some perhaps from you and me.

There are, of course, a number of obstacles in the way of a policy that lays emphasis upon preventing drugs being produced overseas and imported into Britain. One problem, and one that is frequently overlooked in popular debates about drugs, is that many illegal drugs are manufactured in this country, amphetamines are one example. The production, distribution and consumption of amphetamines does currently appear to be increasing in at least some parts of Britain (in the mid-to-late 1980s). The drug is not without its dangers, and some readers will remember the saying, 'speed kills', from the 1960s.

Tranquillizer abuse increased in the 1980s, partly due to increasing availability, and dependence on these drugs is now widely acknowledged (Lader, 1980). Last and not least, there are alcohol and cigarettes.

4.6 DRUG CONTROL AND PROFESSIONAL PRACTICE

IDENTIFYING YOUR INVOLVEMENT IN DRUG CONTROLS

This section will help you identify your own relationship to formal systems of drug control in Britain.

ACTIVITY 4.5
CONTROL AND YOUR WORK

Spend up to 40 minutes on this activity.

(a) Which, if any, of the systems of control, are you involved in *or most likely to be involved in?* Tick the one that applies to you:

● health and welfare system; may sometimes refer drug-using patients or clients to specialist drug agencies, including DDUs
● police, magistrates, jury members, probation, prison staff; may sometimes play a part in putting into prison drug-using persons who may have been convicted of other (i.e. non-drug) offences; or may be involved in a diversion programme that results in drug users going into a rehabilitation programme in preference to prison?
● police and customs engaged in pursuit of suppliers and major traffickers, capture of whom may result in lengthy prison sentences.

(b) Taking one case of your involvement in the formal systems of control of drugs and drug users – *or, if you have no such involvement, choosing any case reported by colleagues or in the local or national media* – try to identify, on a piece of paper:

● the way in which this particular case came to light
● the benefits and the costs, for the individual concerned, for the agency doing the controlling, and for the public at large, of the control action taken

● whether on balance, and in your opinion, the control action was in this case worthwhile (for example, in reducing the various problems in a cost-effective way) or whether it was counter-productive (say, by worsening the situation for one or more 'actors' in the situation) or perhaps a mixed result (good for some people, bad for others).

What modifications, if any, can you identify as desirable in this part of the drug control system?

Comment

You may have found this activity difficult. It is not easy to separate out costs and benefits as different 'actors' may have different perceptions about what is a benefit, or whether a cost is justifiable. There are likely to be as many different interpretations of 'worthwhile' as there were views on penalties for trafficking and supply!

YOUR ROLE IN RELATION TO YOUNG PEOPLE, COLLEAGUES AND OTHER AGENCIES

So far we have been looking at drug controls from a broad social policy perspective. A quite different way of approaching the question of formal drug control is to say, 'Never mind about the question of whether a certain level of penalty is effective in restraining or diminishing the problem overall, how does the law enforcement system impinge upon my own work with people who may be using drugs, and what are the practical implications for how I do my job (or voluntary work etc.)?'

This section of the chapter provides a means of working through this question.

Responding to individuals and situations

Consider the following scenario.

Jo is the type of teenager who never – touch wood – gets into the sorts of nightmare situations that make parents panic, social workers groan and politicians pontificate.

But at 9.30 pm tonight, Friday, a situation was uncovered that might or might not blow up into a major and public problem.

Just as Jo was leaving the Youth Club, laughing with a group of friends, the youth worker heard what she thought was a reference to heroin. She joked along with the group, saying, 'There are times when I feel like giving you lot a smack, too, especially when you won't let me lock up on time!' This way of showing the group that she had indeed picked up something which she was being half-invited to hear succeeded in opening up the topic in a non-threatening way. Out came the story! It seemed that the group were intending to pick up a couple of bottles and cans from the off-licence, and then were likely to move on to the waste land where one, at least, would also sniff glue.

The youth worker – by now long delayed and with her own children waiting to be picked up from a neighbour – made a direct challenge to the group's plans, pointing out (a) her moral position (what would yours be?) and, (b) that mixing sedative-type drugs, such as glue and alcohol, involves a high risk of overdose. This response was well taken by the group, who appreciated her concern. Jo, however, was uncomfortable and defensive. Finally Jo faced the youth worker squarely, saying, 'OK, but at least we don't take smack, do we?' This, the worker remembered, was where the conversation started. There was then a chorus of contradictory statements from the group, with much digging in the ribs, meaningful looks and diversionary remarks. The group dispersed in some confusion, with only Jo hanging around. When the others were at the corner, Jo asked to talk to the worker 'sometime soon, but not now, right?', and then scooted off to catch up with the others.

Jo and the youth worker did chat the following Monday. Jo confided about going drinking with the group, but said that all of them had (on this occasion at least) heeded the worker's advice about mixing their sedatives, and had decided to 'leave it out' as far as solvent sniffing was concerned. Jo's underlying concern with heroin then surfaced. A cousin had smoked the drug on two occasions, and had recommended it to Jo as 'great'. What did the youth worker think? 'I mean, I know you're going to say its bad, and I know that, but what do you really think?'

ACTIVITY 4.6
PERSONALIZING THE ISSUE

Having read the scenario above, spend no more than 30 minutes 'tailoring' it to fit the sorts of young people with whom you are familiar. Make some notes on a piece of paper.

Who is 'Jo'? Decide:

● whether Jo is a young woman or young man?

● whether Jo is white or some other specific ethnic group?

● what social class is Jo?

● what are his/her cultural interests?

● what community expectations are there of the roles and responsibilities of young people such as Jo?

Having put some flesh on the bare bones of the scenario, read it through again, and identify the main issues as you see them. It may be helpful to see if you can identify issues under the following headings:

Legal issues – for the worker Rights and responsibilities under law; responsibilities in relation to individual young people; wider groups of young people who the worker may not know well; might the club get closed down; might the worker get fired?

Legal issues – for young people What are the chances of getting into trouble with the law for use of (a) alcohol, (b) solvents, (c) heroin and other illegal drugs? What are the likely consequences, good and bad? What are the possible consequences of successful evasion of the law, good and bad?

Health issues – avoiding death What are the most dangerous practices in relation to the use of intoxicants such as alcohol, solvents and illegal drugs? Identify possible dangers of death due to (a) overdose (and choking to death or heart failure), and (b) accident (e.g. falling).

Health issues – longer term dangers What are the dangers of becoming dependent on the various intoxicants mentioned in the scenario? What other dangers are there?

Psychological and social dangers What dangers are there in relation to the personal development of Jo and friends? And what about the ways in which other people in the community, parents especially, may respond? Is there a danger of over-reaction and unnecessary labelling from some quarters – or is the danger one of under-reaction and 'turning a blind eye'.

The problem of pleasure How can one respond to the claim that some drug use is 'great', pleasureable? Is it sufficient to say that such pleasure is always followed by a greater pain, or is it necessary to get to grips with the question of what pleasure actually means to the young person concerned? Can you and s/he speak about this?

Using these headings as a checklist, now write down what you think are the most important issues for the youth worker to deal with, in relation to Jo and friends:

● during the *next 5 minutes* (responding to young people at that time)

● during the *next few days* (getting in touch with colleagues and maybe other professions, maybe the parents, to discuss or refer the young people as 'cases' to other agencies)

● during the *next month* (possibly raise the broader issues with management for guidance, or call for training, or press for inter-agency links, or campaign for resources for alternative pleasures for young people . . .?)

The Issues

Your ideas about the issues raised by the 'Jo' scenario so far . . . (you may want to make a larger chart!)

	Over the next 5 minutes	Over the next few days	Over the next month
Legal issues			
Health issues			
Social/ psychological			
Pleasure			

Having identified the main issues of concern in the 'Jo' scenario, let us now move on to consider the ways in which these general issues arise for specific professional groups, and the ways in which different professions try to co-operate to solve the problems. Because individual professions see problems rather differently, and because they have different opportunities for and constraints upon their actions, inter-agency co-operation is not always smooth and effortless.

This second part of the scenario looks at some of the possible conflicts that can arise.

Inter-agency and community co-operation

It is now six weeks since the drinking, solvent sniffing and alleged heroin use first came to light. The youth worker who first talked to Jo's group about these issues has now also talked with her immediate colleagues, putting forward an account of the issues in the terms discussed above (legal, health, pleasure, etc.) As a result of these discussions between colleagues, action was taken on three fronts.

(a) Training   The full-time youth workers decided that they needed a specific time set aside for training to discuss factual information and questions of practice. Due to lack of resources, no 'cover' was available to supervise the youth club in the absence of the full-time workers, and it was felt better to close the club for one night rather than exclude any of the workers from training. So, next Friday, a three-hour training session was conducted with the aid of other workers (club and detached) who had a longer experience of responding to drug problems.

(b) Multi-disciplinary conference   One of the issues that came up on the training night was the question of to what extent other agencies and professions should be liased with over this problem. It was agreed that two of the workers should raise this issue with management, and suggest that the issue be discussed at a meeting of the inter-agency Drugs Advisory Committee in the Borough. This culminated in a Borough-wide interdisciplinary conference in which the Social Services, the Intermediate Treatment Team, the police and a psychiatrist were the main movers. The Jo incident had started a ball rolling, and it was now well down the rocky road of inter-agency action on drugs.

(c) Parents group makes claims   After the conference, there were protests from a hitherto unknown Parents Action Against Drug Abuse group. Furious at being left out of the conference altogether, PAADA spokespersons accused all the professionals of arrogance and of ignorance ('We've been dealing with these problems for two years – now you wake up and think you're experts!'). They also accused the police of inaction and demanded resources from 'the government'. Professionals who had just earlier been at each other's throats now jointly recoiled in horror at PAADA's intervention.

ACTIVITY 4.7
CO-OPERATION, CONFLICTS AND CONTRADICTIONS IN INTERVENTIONS

Spend about 30 minutes on this activity.

Take a role   At this point you should take the role, in your imagination, of one of the professional groups represented at the multi-disciplinary conference. (You can be yourself/own profession, or you can experiment with trying to see things from the perspective of one of the other professions). The professions include:

social worker; GP; psychiatrist; teacher; youth worker; probation officer; nurse; health visitor; police (community or juvenile liaison, drug squad or uniformed).

Choose which profession are you going to be, and at what level of seniority (trainee, basic grade, senior, etc.). Note this down.

Work out your professional position in an area of contradictions and conflicts.   Here are a number of inter-professional conflicts that emerged from the Borough multi-disciplinary conference. Take *just one* of these, referring to the resources provided, work out where you stand today. (Remember, you are free to change your mind as the course goes on.)

The issue of the record system   At the conference, the police and Social Services describe a system of keeping records on young people thought to be in contact with drugs or solvent sniffing. They criticize certain detached youth workers for failing to pass on to them information on young people suspected of using cannabis and other drugs. There are counter-claims of police heavy-handedness and racism (especially in relation to police relations with the local Afro-Caribbean community). The psychiatrist tries to steer a middle course, acknowledging youth workers and other professionals' need to keep the trust of their clients, but backing the police in their efforts to get information to catch local drug dealers.

Note down Where do you stand on the question of a record system? Is it useful, or dangerous? If it has to be kept, then what should be the involvements and responsibilities of your own profession – and what safeguards should be built in? Should any drug record system that carries unconfirmed data be available to parents, if they demand this?

The issue of the court diversion programme At the conference, the Intermediate Treatment team describe the idea of a 'diversion programme' to provide alternatives to court appearances for young persons at risk to drug use. They want to set up such a service locally, providing counselling and community service for young people who might otherwise develop a career in the criminal justice system. This is strongly supported by some at the conference. Others, however, have worries: they stress the rights of the individual to be judged as a person responsible for their actions, and criticize it and similar programmes for soaking up resources that should, they say, go into mainstream leisure and recreational facilities for all.

Note down What do you think should happen to a young person suspected of illegal drug use: placed into the criminal justice system for adjudication; or into a diversion programme; or some other method of 'disposal' used; or no formal control action at all?

The issue of policing policy The entry into the drug debate by PAADA, the parents group, puts the police on the defensive. Egged on by the local newspaper, PAADA claims that the police's commitment to catching drug dealers is more a matter of rhetoric than accomplishment. There are allegations that names and addresses of 'known dealers' have been passed to the police on several occasions, yet no arrests or even searches followed. The police defend their record, saying that they are seeking to trace the sources of supply – the 'top people'. They say that they could give no further details for fear of alerting their prey. There are conflicting demands upon the law enforcement system at the conference, and in the local press. Some people call for the government to introduce hanging, others call for the legalization of drugs, and there are many shades of opinion in between.

Note down As far as you are concerned, as a professional meeting people who sometimes use illegal drugs, solvents, alcohol or prescribed drugs and who sometimes have problems associated with this drug use, how would you like to see the police act? Should the police focus upon particular types of drugs; or leave your clients alone; or intervene more vigorously and take these clients off your books?

Comment

Now that you have begun to work through some collaborative policies on drug misuse you might like to develop these further and work with colleagues to plan an inter-agency policy on drugs.

4.7 CONCLUSION

The question remains as persistent as ever – what *can* be done about drug control?

This chapter has offered no easy answer, because there is none. It seems certain that Britain will continue to have drug problems – around imported drugs, other drugs that are illegal but produced in this country, and the various legal intoxicants and medicines – for many years. The question of how the practitioner can respond, what part s/he will play in drug control at the level of his or her professional practice, remains on the table.

We hope that we have helped you to define your views about several aspects of drug control:

● the history (what lessons does it offer us for drug control today?)

● current policy issues (the most effective ways of organizing law enforcement and treatment)

● questions of practice (what to do when faced with an immediate problem, who else to tell, how to work with other agencies).

These questions summarize the agenda for action on drug control. Being able to formulate the questions is halfway (well, maybe a third of the way) towards getting good answers.

REFERENCES

Bewley, T. (1969) 'Control of Drugs and Dependence', *The Medico: Legal Journal* Vol 371 pp. 7–17

British Medical Association Professional Division/Action on Alcohol Abuse (1986) *Comparative Mortality from Drugs of Addiction,* British Medical Association

Dorn, N. (1983) *Alcohol, Youth and the State,* Croom Helm

Gooberman, L. (1974) *Operation Intercept: The multiple consequences of public policy,* Pergamon

Helmer, J. (1975) *Drugs and Minority Oppression,* Seabury Press

Helmer, J. & Vietorisz, T. (1974) *Drug use, the Labour Market and Class Conflict,* Drug Abuse Council

Inglis, B. (1975) *The Forbidden Game: a social history of drugs,* Hodder and Stoughton

Inglis, B. (1976) *The Opium War,* Coronet Books

Lader, M. (1980) 'The Mindbenders (2): Tranquillisers and Sleeping Pills', *Mind Out,* July/August, 41, pp. 19–20

Taylor, P. (1984) *Smoke Ring: the politics of tobacco,* Bodley Head

Teff, H. (1973) *Legal and Social Aspects of Drug Dependence,* University of London: PhD thesis

The Wootton Report (UK Advisory Committee on Drug Dependence) (1968) *Cannabis,* HMSO

FURTHER READING

If you would like to learn more about some of the issues raised in this chapter we suggest you read Dorn, N. & South, N. (eds.) *A Land Fit for Heroin?: Drug Policies, Prevention and Practice,* Macmillan, 1987.

5 INTERVENTION APPROACHES

5.1 INTRODUCTION

In previous chapters we have looked at the complex influences at work when an individual starts experimenting with, and using, drugs. We have also discussed societal approaches towards the control of such drug usage. Clearly the personal desires of an individual to use drugs may conflict with society's control measures. This conflict, in turn, will set the context for the establishment of various facilities for intervention and the way in which the individual may be directed towards, or seek out, help to stop or reduce drug usage. Choice of a service will depend on many factors, for instance, type and severity of the problem, knowledge of the service and its availability and reputation amongst other drug users. In many instances users may also approach their general practitioner and/or generic services such as the probation service, youth service, social services, community nursing service, Samaritans, Citizens Advice Bureau, etc. They may also seek the support of family, partner, friends or neighbours to help them at particular stages of their drug use.

This chapter will explore the range of interventions currently offered, and the particular philosophies on which these intervention services are based.

5.2 DRUG USE AND PROBLEM USE

Drug use in itself does not necessarily imply a drug problem. For some, it is a matter of experiment and adolescent risk taking. For others it will be an occasional social activity. In other instances it is a regular controlled activity. For a minority, it is a total, indiscriminate involvement. The legal status of the drug used is only one factor. How much is used, how often, by what route it is consumed and, perhaps most significantly, the importance the user attaches to the drug used are all factors in determining the type of help which services offer to the individual.

ACTIVITY 5.1
YOUR OWN TYPES OF USE

Spend 15 minutes on this activity.

In Activity 2.2 (Chapter 2) you made a note of the drugs you currently use. Look back at this activity, then note, on a separate sheet of paper, the drugs you listed in Activity 2.2. Add to the list other drugs that you have tried at least once.

Using the categories we have described above – experimental/occasional/recreational/indiscriminate – categorize your drug use. For each of the drugs you have listed note a category of use.

Comment

You may be an experimental drug user – 'try this drink and see what you think'. Or an occasional user – 'I like a cigar on special occasions'. Or a regular drug user – 'I usually have a drink with my evening meal'. You may even have a problem drug use – 'I can't get by without a cigarette!'

We use drugs for different reasons on different occasions – as a social lubricant; to relax after a hard day; to keep going. We are also occasional casualties of drugs (tobacco and alcohol) which can result in bronchitis, heart disease, accidents. We overdose – are sick, have a hangover. In fact, much of our behaviour is not too dissimilar to that of drug users who are our present cause for concern.

Think about figures for deaths and injuries from drinking alcohol (you may want to look back at Chapter 3, Section 3.2). In dealing with drug use, the difference we have to come to terms with is between socially acceptable and socially unacceptable behaviour. In that process, we have to come to terms with our own drug use and what is acceptable – and what is unacceptable about someone else's drug use. Your view on drug acceptability will be influenced by the position you take in the 'abstinence versus harm reduction' debate. The next section explores these two stances.

5.3   ABSTINENCE OR HARM REDUCTION?

It is useful to group the services into broad categories according to their objectives and broad theoretical underpinnings. Some are abstinence oriented, with the central goal of assisting the drug user to become and/or remain drug free. Others operate on the basis of harm reduction, trying to reduce the damage which can arise from drug use – for these services, abstinence may be one, but not the only acceptable outcome. The final group of services is for parents and relatives of drug users. These services may be abstinence or harm reduction oriented, but are essentially concerned with assisting parents, relatives and, in many instances, the local community cope with the problems of drug use as they affect them.

ABSTINENCE ORIENTED SERVICES

The central theme of these services is that the individual cannot function as a complete person unless they become and remain drug free. However, there are significant differences in the definition of drugs and the theoretical underpinnings of these services. These reflect a long-standing debate in both the alcohol and drug fields about the nature of addiction. For some, the dependent use of alcohol and drugs is considered an illness/disease whilst for others it is representative of a personality disorder which can be corrected and resolved through therapeutic intervention. The central focus of treatment approaches in both instances is abstinence from drugs, which are seen as replacing personal/biological deficiency in the individual. A number of treatment modes prevail. The key features of the principal ones are shown in the figure opposite.

HARM REDUCTION ORIENTED SERVICES

Services designed to achieve harm reduction use a variety of theoretical models. In many instances, the models used are unstated or are mixtures of various approaches from different disciplines. They are more commonly involved with a wide range of drug users, from experimental to indiscriminate. Many will incorporate theoretical models from the abstinence oriented services within the scope of their approach to individuals. There are, however, some more distinct models which they use. A model gaining increasing popularity is the social problem/social casualty model which sees drug use as a feature of deficits in the environment, rather than the individual. Another model, risk taking, cites drug use as a feature of normal adolescent behaviour. Key features of both models are shown in the figure.

MODELS OF DRUG DEPENDENCY

DISEASE MODEL 1

- Some individuals are physiologically and psychologically susceptible to various substances
- Once started there is an inevitable decline into total dependence
- The 'disease' of addiction is incurable and stays with the individual for life
- Whilst an individual may prefer a particular drug (say, heroin), use of any drug (say, alcohol) will precipitate decline and return to original dependence
- The course of the 'disease' can only be arrested by lifelong abstinence from taking drugs, including alcohol

PERSONALITY DISORDER MODEL

- Drug users have a distorted personality which leads to dependence
- They use drugs as a way of resolving/avoiding personal conflicts
- Techniques of self-awareness and self-management can be taught. They can then sort out their personality and reduce their need for drugs
- Drug treatment comes into the realm of psychiatry and mental health

SPIRITUAL PROBLEM MODEL

- Drugs are used to fill a void left by a lack of spiritual and religious values
- Abstinence from drugs is essential to allow for proper spiritual development
- Evangelical communities can help develop spiritual awareness and thus reduce the need for drug use

DISEASE MODEL 2

- Drug addiction is a manifestation of disease and not merely a form of vicious indulgence
- The drug is taken not for the purposes of obtaining positive pleasure, but in order to relieve a morbid and overpowering craving
- For most drug addicts, gradual withdrawal from their drug of dependence will be successful and they will be able to resume a normal life
- Some people, while capable of leading a useful and fairly normal life so long as they take a certain non-progressive quantity of the drug of addiction, cease to be able to do so when the drug is withdrawn
- Addiction for this small group is controllable through the prescription of a stable supply of the drug of addiction
- The medical model of treatment and the clinic system was based on this philosophy. In the 1970s this was largely replaced by the personality disorder/social problem model. In some areas it is now being revived as a harm reduction model, seeking to persuade drug users away from illicit heroin into a less harmful and more controlled pattern of drug use

SOCIAL PROBLEM MODEL

- Drug misuse is a response to social problems
- The user is a social casualty, not a deficient person
- Unemployment, poor working conditions, social environment etc., are key factors in precipitating and maintaining drug use
- People can be helped to make changes in their own circumstances which make drug use less important/necessary
- Drug use and treatment comes into the political and community development arena

RISK TAKING MODEL

- Drug taking is a feature of adolescent development
- Drugs are part of the risk taking that occurs during the change to adulthood
- Experimenters with drugs are not abnormal; if given alternatives they will choose them
- Helping drug users relies on the provision of activity oriented services, youth and community work, etc.

ACTIVITY 5.2a
DISEASE OR SOCIAL CASUALTY?

Allow 20 minutes for this activity.

In disease models, it is believed that certain people are particularly vulnerable to some substances i.e. alcohol, psychotropic drugs. Two variations on the disease model are shown in the figure on p. 63: they have similar characteristics but different treatment strategies. You were introduced to the model in Chapter 1 and asked to work on the paper in the Reader by Heather and Robertson. Find this activity and your response. Spend a few minutes thinking about things you might want to add to your list as a result of working through the course so far. Now read the paper again. When you have done so write a brief statement on your view of the usefulness of the model as a way of explaining problem drug use.

Comment

Before we comment we would like you to think more about the notion of social casualty. This is discussed by Griffiths Edwards in section one of the Course Reader. You may wish to read this article now.

ACTIVITY 5.2b

Look back at Chapter 3, Section, 3.2 where Pearson discusses Plant's finding that young men from lower class homes had increased alcohol consumption. When you have done so write a brief statement on your view of the usefulness of the social casualty model as a way of explaining problem drug use.

Comment

Heather and Robertson suggest that the disease model has been widely accepted, although it is not grounded in solid scientific research. 'Disease/deficiency models, because they place responsibility solely with the individual rather than within a range of contributing factors to drug using behaviour, are increasingly felt to be too narrow a response.'

Perhaps the greatest problem with the disease model is that it concentrates on those relatively few individuals with major problems, and sees the rest of the population as 'normal'. Disease Model 1 sees the disease as arrestable but incurable whilst Disease Model 2 sees the disease as normally curable but for the minority, incurable but non-progressive.

It can be argued that the mass population would benefit from reducing drugs use (particularly alcohol and tobacco). A harm reduction approach might advocate sensible drinking, rather than no drinking, for example. This wider, health promotion approach will be discussed in Chapter 7.

The notion of social casualty reduces the sole burden of responsibility for drug use from individuals and locates it across a wide range of influencing factors (housing, employment, leisure policies/opportunities, personal relationships etc.). The individual is thus empowered to change influencing factors on use, rather than use being the central focus of attention. Chapter 6 explores some of the strategies that are used.

ACTIVITY 5.3
WHAT MODEL EXPLAINS YOUR USE?

Spend 5 minutes on this activity.

In Activity 5.1 you noted down drugs that you currently use, or have used in the past. Look back at the associated figure and the five models shown. Is there one or more that you would choose to explain your use?

Comment

It is possible that you will have chosen one or other of the harm reduction models as these allow a greater degree of freedom of choice than the abstinence based models. Disease/deficit models, because they blame the victim rather than identify the causes of using behaviours, are increasingly being recognized as too narrow a response. This is not to decry the value of some of the strategies used however. These will be discussed, together with services offered, in the next section.

5.4 SERVICES FOR DRUG USERS

Services for drug users have developed in the UK over the last 20 years. As well as describing them by the model which they use, they can be defined by the period in which they developed, by whether they are run by health/local authorities or voluntary organizations and by the treatment philosophies on which they are based.

In Chapter 4 (Activity 4.2) you worked through a Reader paper by Stimson and noted the main changes that have occurred in intervention approaches from the 1960s to the present. Changes identified were as follows:

● In the 1960s the British Clinic model of treatment, based on the disease model, was at its supremacy.

● In the 1970s users were encouraged to take responsibility for their drug taking behaviour, and therapeutic contracts were introduced as a basis for treatment.

● The 1980s saw the decline of the clinic system and the rise of community (voluntary) responses to problem drug use:
(a) There was a shift from viewing users as being addicted (and requiring medical intervention) towards recognizing drug problems as multi-faceted and needing a number of different types of response.
(b) This shift led to an increasing number of generalists in the field, and requirements for greater inter-agency working.

You may wish to look back at this paper now.

**ACTIVITY 5.4
SERVICES FOR USERS**

Allow 30 minutes for this activity.

The characteristics of different helping agencies are described by Strang in the Reader article 'Community initiatives in drug treatment'. One of the services that Strang describes is the community drugs team. Some characteristics of these teams are:

● that they are mainly staffed by professional workers (social workers/community psychiatric nurses)

● that they aim at early intervention in a drug using career

● that they act as a resource and 'back up' for other generic services.

Now read this article, and as you do so, note down characteristics of each of the intervention services described.

Comment

The characteristics of particular services are shown in the figure overleaf. Before looking at this, however, it is worth picking up some other points made by Strang. He, like Stimson, notes that drug services in the UK have been provided with very little thought of evaluation; treatment policies proceed largely without empirical investigation. Bear this in mind as you work through the rest of this chapter and Chapter 6.

Strang notes that a wide range of services are provided, and that this breadth of response is necessary: there is no single adequate response. In discussing specialist services and community services he notes that it is in the community that the problem exists, and it is to the community that the user has to return. He concludes, however, that it is not a question of either specialist service or community service, rather it is a question of the proportion of each that needs to be provided in response.

As you read through the figure overleaf you will see that, generally, there is a move away from adopting rigid approaches/solutions and a move towards combining a range of approaches. This is particularly noticeable in the hospital services, where a move towards a harm reduction approach is now apparent. A study by Mitcheson and Hartnoll conducted at University College Hospital, London provided the stimulus for substantial changes in the approach of hospital services. In this study, drug users attending the hospital for drug treatment were randomly allocated to receive a prescription

SERVICES FOR DRUG USERS

HOSPITAL BASED SERVICES

- Initially based on Disease Model 2/personality disorder models. Placed treatment within medicine and psychiatry
- Offers medical treatment: detoxification–short-, medium-, or long-term methadone prescribing; individual and group therapy. Also begun to adopt elements of the social problem model
- May be the basis of the District or Regional Drug Problem Team
- No specific length of treatment, although out-patient detoxification is normally for no more than six months and may be considerably less. Treatment after detoxification is dependent on the needs of the individual
- Aims to assist drug user to control and contain drug use through provision of legal prescription and to move away from use of illicit drugs towards abstinence
- May co-ordinate community based treatment package or refer to other specialist services for specific treatments/rehabilitation
- Appears to be most used by people dependent on opioids

STREET AGENCIES

- Based on social problem model. Offer day centres/shelters/telephone counselling/'drop in' services
- Are users' advocates
- Use is seen as a social/personal problem: there is a strong element of social work
- Often the service which has first contact with the drug user. Aims to reduce harm arising from drug use and related lifestyle
- Aims to provide treatment and rehabilitation package through co-ordinating the input of other services and through referral to other services according to individual needs
- May cater for specific client groups: young/unemployed/women
- Help co-ordinate work of other agencies
- Offer training and support for other agencies

RESIDENTIAL SERVICES

ABSTINENCE BASED

DISEASE MODEL

- Sometimes called 'Minnesota model'; based on Disease Model 1
- Usually aimed at total abstinence: incorporates principles of AA/NA into programme
- Usually 8–10 weeks residence plus attendance at local AA/NA meetings
- Uses self-help/group discussion etc. Encourages family involvement/support
- Appears to work best for people who have not lost all usual social support systems (family/job etc.)

SPIRITUAL PROBLEM MODEL

- Based on disordered personality due to spiritual void
- Therapeutic religious communities: normal length of stay is 12 months
- Variety of techniques used; may borrow from other approaches
- May be encouraged to attend bible study/prayers etc.

SELF HELP GROUPS

USER GROUPS

- Frequently based on disease/spiritual problem models–members concede that they are powerless over their addiction (Alcoholics/Narcotics Anonymous etc.)
- Often develop because problems of drug dependence not recognized/met by existing services, i.e. TRANX formed to help women reduce dependence on medically prescribed tranquillizers/anti-depressants (based on social casualty theory)
- Users help each other by support/counselling/group work
- Some groups (influenced by the 'Junkies Union' in the Netherlands) work with people who are still using. These groups have had minimal impact in the UK

PARENTS/PARTNERS/RELATIVES/FRIENDS

- Different theoretical models used
- Mutual support provided in order that effective ways of responding to problem drug use in the family can develop: Families Anonymous teach the concept of 'tough love'

COMMUNITY DRUGS TEAMS

- Use social problem model. Mostly professionals: social workers/community psychiatric nurses
- Aid and support community responses to a problem. Operate as a resource and 'back up' for other generic services
- Individual counselling and development work aims at early intervention/rehabilitation/referral
- May be problems if staff employed and managed by different agencies: conflicting treatment philosophies

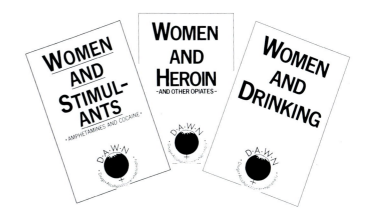

HARM REDUCTION BASED

PERSONALITY DISORDER MODEL

- Sometimes called 'concept houses' (concept based therapeutic communities)
- Based on AA principles: strict hierarchical internal structure/residents earn increasing responsibility within the structure
- Normal stay is around 12–15 months. Last 4–6 months may be 're-entry' preparation for independent living
- Groupwork challenges negative attitudes; psycho drama helps develop social and personal skills
- Appears to be more effective for those with little social support/life previously dominated by drug use

SOCIAL PROBLEM MODEL

- Democratically run communities—length of stay flexible
- Process of running the house co-operatively encourages the development of personal and life skills
- Counselling and group work aimed at planning strategies to avoid further drug use/developing relationships with the wider community

COMMUNITY AND VOLUNTEER GROUPS

- Developed from parent support groups
- Run by volunteers/local people—may not have professional advice/training (this can be seen by some users as an advantage!)
- Offer telephone counselling/'drop-in'/crisis call-out services
- Can have good relationships/contacts with other agencies

for either heroin or oral methadone. 'The results in summary, were that those receiving heroin, with the exception of their illicit drug use, changed very little in their behaviour whilst those receiving methadone either became more heavily involved in drug use and drug using groups or became significantly less involved and moved towards abstinence.'

This study provided evidence of what was already occurring, that is, the move away from the prescription of injectable drugs to oral drugs and from heroin to methadone. The advantages were seen as taking away encouragement to a particularly risky form of drug administration, injection; using a drug which was longer acting and which could reduce the centrality of drug use to the user's life; providing room for other, more therapeutic interventions with the individual; utilizing more effectively the expensive skills of the specialist staff in the drug treatment service.

The change also signalled a move in the theoretical underpinnings of these services. They had been based on a medical/psychiatric model assuming an illness and personal pathology concept, they now started to shift towards a model which recognized social problems and influences. In effect, they adapted the models used in the abstinence oriented therapeutic communities for use in non-residential settings.

The hospital-based services now largely operate on the basis of short- and medium-term prescribing of oral methadone as a programme of out-patient detoxification, combined with group and individual counselling, and integrated into other community services to create a treatment 'package'. There has been little development of hospital-based in-patient services, perhaps because the location and consequent restrictions have given little flexibility for developing programmes for a group of patients who are essentially young, and after drug withdrawal, healthy and active.

Another philosophical shift, apparent in a number of approaches, is that of treating drug use as part of, not the main focus of, everyday living. This is frequently related to a programme of personal and social development of the user, enabling them to become more in control of their own lifestyle.

ACTIVITY 5.5
USERS' VIEWS ON
INTERVENTION APPROACHES

Spend 20 minutes on this activity.

In the section of the audio cassette associated with this chapter you will hear some drug users and workers talking about intervention approaches. Play the cassette. As you listen write a short paragraph about what you think is seen as particularly helpful/unhelpful about the interventions discussed.

Comment

Kate rejected the approach offered by Alcoholics Anonymous because she did not want the organization 'dominating her life'. She did not see this as any real advance on alcohol dominating her life. For Kate the spiritual aspect was also unimportant. She has a successful career and has a strong, long-term relationship with her boyfriend. She also has a strong personality and prefers to negotiate treatment with one known counsellor. Her immediate goal is abstinence (to remain 'dry') but she anticipates that, at some stage in the future, she may be able to drink alcohol occasionally.

The special problems of helping alcohol users were discussed by Doug who also spoke of the limitations of the disease model of treatment. He believes that client-determined services (community alcohol teams) are especially attractive because they allow for a range of treatment interventions – different ways of 'putting the ceiling back up'. They also focus on what is possible, rather than what is not.

Low self-esteem was cited by both Brian and Carol when talking about the approach of a therapeutic community. A first step in building esteem is to make the new entrant user feel valued. Carol found this very difficult, initially, and was not able to work successfully within the community until she had done some 'facing up to the past'. Doing this allowed her to form new relationships and take on new responsibilities.

PATTERNS OF PROVISION

From the brief descriptions of the specialist services provided for people with drug problems, you will seen that there is a wide variety of approaches to services. There is also variation in the availability of these services. The range of services in any one area may be radically different from that which is available in another area. There is no standard pattern, but rather an attempt in some areas to create a pattern out of the *ad hoc* development of services which already exist.

ACTIVITY 5.6
SERVICES IN YOUR AREA

We cannot put a time on this activity – it may need to be done in several stages.

In Activity 1.6 (optional) you were asked to build up a picture of drug use in your area. You may have used services to help you to do this. Now we want you to think about service provision. In this chapter we have been talking about changes in philosophy and service provision; how recent is your knowledge of the range, type, and characteristics of services provided?

Find out what services are available for people with drug problems in your area. How easy is it to find help? In finding out, talk, if you can, with users as well as providers of services. How accessible and acceptable is service provision? Try to decide what gaps in services there are and then list them in order of priority of filling these needs.

Comment

You should have identified at least some information about services, although it may not have been easy. Looking at the way you went about finding a service may suggest ways in which people seek help, and may provide an insight into the need to make services accessible, not just 'user friendly' when they have been found. Assessing the gaps in services and listing them in order of priority should help you further identify your own approach to drug problems and prompt you to look at it again, perhaps exploring how other, non-drug services might play an effective part in making up the local pattern of services.

5.5 INTERVENTION PROBLEMS

Drug use continues to present new problems, or old problems in new guises. A very recent area of concern has been the high risk to drug users who inject drugs and share injection equipment that they might be infected by the AIDS virus (HIV – Human Immuno-deficiency Virus). The debate about how to respond to this problem has raised a variety of additional problems, in particular, whether harm reduction or total abstinence should be the goal. On the one hand, it is argued that injection equipment should be made available to drug users to reduce the chance that equipment will be shared and therefore that infection will be spread. On the other hand, it is argued that this condones continued drug use and does not *prevent* unhygienic injection practices. In another guise, this is a repeat of arguments about the use of long-term prescribing of methadone against short-term/no prescribing in order to detoxify and achieve abstinence. One concentrates on the individual and his/her present interaction with society, the other concentrates on the individual to achieve long-term change which will consequentially benefit society.

5.6   CONCLUSIONS

In this chapter, we have discussed the range of services available for people with drug problems, explored your own responses to drug use and the model you have of drug users, and recognized that a variety of responses are needed. If there is one certainty in the response to drug problems, it is that if someone or some service says they have *the* answer, you can say with confidence, they're wrong.

The difficulty of finding the 'right' intervention for users has been raised in this chapter. In addition to finding a successful intervention approach there is also the need to develop an effective working relationship with the user, in which both the personal drug career, and willingness to change it are recognized. Practitioner characteristics may be as influential as user characteristics in determining a successful outcome. These themes will be discussed in Chapter 6.

REFERENCE

Mitcheson, M. & Hartnoll, R. 'Conflicts in deciding treatment within drug dependency clinics' in *Problems of Drug Abuse in Britain* – papers presented to the Cropwood Round Table Conference, Dec. 1977, D. J. West (ed.), University of Cambridge, Institute of Criminology, 1978.

6 TREATMENT SKILLS

6.1 INTRODUCTION

In Chapter 5 you were introduced to the range of interventions currently available and the contending influences of abstinence and harm reduction philosophies behind the development of services. In this chapter we look at the expectations that the practitioner and drug user bring into the intervention situation.

Before we proceed, however, it is important to note that there is considerable uncertainty about the effects of the various treatments currently available to users. In their review of research Raistrick and Davidson (1985, in the Reader), for example, conclude that current research raises many questions about the effectiveness of modern treatments. They say that evidence suggests that different treatments, however defined, are not qualitatively different from the natural way in which people change their drug using habits. Nevertheless, although no treatment approach seems to be superior to others, they do suggest that treatment generally seems to result in a better outcome than no treatment at all. Bearing this in mind this chapter stresses the importance of being clear about the goals that are set during an intervention programme.

Students following this course are expected to have a range of skills useful to working with drug users and this material may help to enhance these skills. However, it is important to note that the material will not make students proficient in the range of helping skills needed when working with drug users.

6.2 INTERVENTIONS

Whatever the philosophy or model behind the treatment approach to drug use – whether this is defined as a disease or as a behaviour disorder – the intervention will aim at changing a practice which, up until then at least, has been presented in some acceptable form. It may be that the drug user will make the first approach for assistance or it may be that the intervention follows the request of others and thus, by implication, goes against the wishes of the user. Most often it will probably be a mixture of the two, with the individual, perhaps somewhat unconvincingly, requesting 'treatment' in order to relieve pressures which have made continued drug use more difficult and less pleasurable.

INTERVENE FOR WHAT?

Decisions to intervene in the life of a particular individual, and the nature of the intervention, therefore, should not simply depend on finding common ground between the attitudes or beliefs of the practitioner and those of the individual. If it is to be successful, it must also be based upon a good understanding of the reasons behind the intervention, whether the drug user has sought help or this has been forced upon him or her.

ACTIVITY 6.1
ADVANTAGES AND DISADVANTAGES OF A HOBBY

This activity is in two parts.

Part 1: *Spend 10 minutes on this part.*
Divide a sheet of paper into two columns. Head the first *Advantages* and the second *Disadvantages*. Now think of an activity, or hobby, to which you have been particularly attached over the years and provide a list of *ten advantages* and *ten disadvantages* that you associate with your

activity or hobby. For example, advantages: it relaxes me; it takes my mind off problems, disadvantages: it encourages me to put off unpleasant tasks; it isolates me from my family, etc. It does not particularly matter what activity you choose to analyse in this way.

Part 2: *Spend 10 minutes on this part*
Now imagine that this activity has been declared illegal and that a series of specialist treatment centres has been established to 'wean sufferers off this debilitating and dangerous habit'. How might you respond? Would you continue your activity in secret? Would you go to the nearest treatment centre straight away? Would you go to the centre to show willing but secretly continue? Would your relationships with family and friends be affected by any of your responses? Make a list of *ten* possible responses and write down the advantage and disadvantage of each.

Comment

In practice, drug treatments are simply geared towards helping individuals resolve similar habits. An added dimension is that this particular habit is illegal. How people respond to pressure on them to stop or modify their habits is unlikely to be clear-cut. It will probably be a muddled cost-benefit analysis involving a balance between advantages and disadvantages, as in the activity.

Unfortunately, the majority of drug specialist agencies do not build their treatment programmes on the assumption that drug users, like anyone faced with pressure to change habits, are likely to be uncertain about their desire for intervention. There seems to be a somewhat crude and unrealistic assumption that some users will become 'motivated' by a sudden flash of insight to stop.

This assumption is obstructive in two major ways:

Firstly, it may discourage the practitioner from questioning the treatment ideology. Often such ideologies become an important part of the practitioner's personal belief system and challenging it, like challenging valued hobbies, can be rather upsetting. If the failure of individual drug users to 'succeed' can be conveniently blamed on a lack of motivation then there is little incen-

tive to do more than tinker with the material nuts and bolts of the system.

Secondly, for the drug user the emphasis on motivation can be similarly convenient. Most efforts to break habits involve several attempts to change before achieving the desired aim. (Many of us will be familiar with the several attempts of smokers to change their habit before they succeed). Looking back on earlier attempts can be painful and embarrassing and it can be a lot simpler, therefore, to blame failure on lack of motivation.

'DRESS REHEARSALS'

Perhaps a better way to face this problem is to encourage drug users to see failures to break their habit as 'dress rehearsals' and as learning experiences for the next time. This approach also encourages practitioners to examine the services they offer and to consider fundamental changes where these do not meet the needs of the drug users.

ACTIVITY 6.2
CHANGING HABITS

Spend 20 minutes on this activity.

Read 'Treatment and change' by Raistrick and Davidson in the Reader. Note what the authors have to say about the process of changing habits and write a paragraph on how the drug user may be influenced by pressure from others in each of the suggested five stages in changing drug using behaviour.

Comment

Raistrick and Davidson refer to Prochaska and Di Clemente's stages of change: *precontemplation* – at this stage the user may be unaware of having a particular problem, or deny it. Pressure to recognize that there is a problem could initially lead to withdrawal and isolation from those who wish to help. *Contemplation* – during this stage the person becomes increasingly aware that there is a problem. It is possible that pressure might lead to further denial and arguments before the drug user decides on action in the *determination* stage

– this may be a relatively short time span and pressure may encourage unrealistic goals with consequent early failure. The *maintenance* stage involves the individual in fairly continuous efforts to maintain the new behaviour before the *termination* stage is reached and use of the drugs has stopped. It is also quite possible, of course, that pressure on a drug user may increase movement through the various stages.

Other factors which need to be borne in mind when considering an appropriate intervention programme involve an examination of the drug user's particular needs and the extent to which meeting these might conflict with social norms, those around the user and the political expectations of the practitioner as someone who 'cures' drug users not 'colludes' with them, etc. While Raistrick and Davidson suggest that there is reason for some optimism in the long term, they point out that not everyone changes their habits at once and it might be useful to think in terms of a treatment career. There is obviously some connection between the idea of passing through stages in the treatment career and the idea of transition points in the drug user career as discussed in Chapter 3.

6.3 PROBLEM ASSESSMENT

The piecemeal evolution of treatment approaches discussed in the previous chapter and the evidence on treatment outcomes from Raistrick and Davidson show that it is important to be much clearer about what is being done and to tailor interventions for the individual.

A BROAD SPECTRUM

Attempts to classify drug use into a limited number of subgroups in order to prescribe appropriate treatments for each has not been fruitful. Drug use cannot be so easily simplified. Dependence seems to be a point at the far end of the spectrum of quite normal behaviour. Most individuals who experience problems of dependence will do so only from time to time.

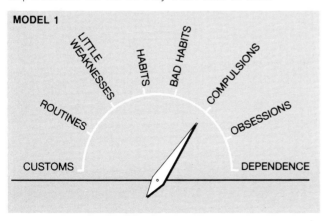

If we imagine drug dependence as a scale much like that in Model 1 this may help to illustrate the way in which drugs of various kinds are normally experienced by the individual. At the lower end of the scale we might find 'customs'. These would include the little things we always do in a particular way because. . .well we've always done it that way. For example, most of us have a favourite side upon which we go to sleep and find it difficult to sleep in any other position. Further up the scale rewards will increase. Some of the things we do may make us feel very good.

There is nothing abnormal about doing something again if it made us feel good before. However, there are some people who, for one reason or another find a particular experience so exciting, so exhilarating, so comforting, that they want to do it all the time or they think about doing it all the time when they're not doing it. They become irritated and restless with other activities which take them away from the pleasurable activity.

As we saw in Chapter 3 dependence can develop over a period of time. Dependence (on drink or drugs or any other comforting experience) is rarely a static affair. The amount we indulge ourselves will depend upon availability, finance, and the right set and setting. The influence of sets and settings was discussed in Chapter 2 where it was argued that particular sets and settings can influence the effects of taking drugs.

ACTIVITY 6.3
INFLUENCE AND COMFORTS

Spend 20 minutes on this.

Return to Activity 6.1 and look at your chosen activity/hobby. Make brief notes on the following questions:

● Has it always been as important?

● Are there times when you do it for 'the wrong reasons'?

● If so, what made it different on those occasions?

● Does it always make you feel the same? Are there times when other things are so interesting and important that you don't do it at all?

Comment

You will probably have found that, although you might see a particular activity or experience as a constant factor in your life, over time it 'ebbs and flows' according to the pressures of other life events.

We have been stressing the complex nature of the decision to use, or stop using, drugs and the difficulty in trying to identify causes and effects without ending up with superficial explanations and encouraging drug users to set unrealistic goals. In the next activity we ask you to examine these issues more closely.

ACTIVITY 6.4
ATTENTION TO DETAIL

Spend 25 minutes on this activity.

Thorley believes that the aim of treatment is to help individuals sort out problems related to drug taking and to look behind superficial explanations. You should now read the Reader article, 'Some practical approaches to the problem drug taker for non-prescribing workers', by Dr Anthony Thorley. While you are doing so pay special attention to his advice on history taking and the value in finding out why a drug user decides to seek, or accept, treatment.

Comment

There are several helpful intervention strategies identified, some concerned with assessment (history) and others with treatment. They are as follows:

History

● Find out what has motivated the user's acceptance of help (the leading edge)

● Learn about the drug taking career

● Identify previous dress rehearsals

● Identify a typical pattern of use

Treatment

● Educate and inform

● Set goals

● Modify consumption

● Rehabilitate

Another framework for looking at the way people become dependent has been suggested by Dr Russell of the Addiction Research Unit (1976). He pointed out that 'the mountain climber who hangs over a 300 foot cliff suspended by a single rope can truly be said to be dependent upon that rope'. But what if the drop is only three feet or if he/she has more than one rope?

The scale in Model 2 is a fairly graphic way of showing how dependence can fluctuate according to a variety of other circumstances and pressures.

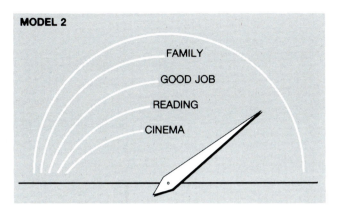

MODEL 2

An effective assessment of problem drug use will take account of the number of 'ropes' a user has available, and their length and strength.

AN ASSESSMENT MODEL

The aim of any constructive intervention is to identify and resolve two distinct and separate sets of problems:

Primary problems – which result directly from the nature of the drug being used, the way the drug is used and societal and familial pressures.

Secondary problems – some drug users may also have a second set of problems which are not directly caused by their drug use. These are problems for which drug taking was originally, or has now become, a solution. For example, those who believe themselves to be in some way inadequate may find comfort in drug use.

In exploring problems which might lie behind an individual's use of drugs, or which might result from it, Model 3 may prove useful in clarifying the issues for both the practitioner and the drug user.

The model assumes three interacting factors in the use of drugs, or any other mood changing experience.

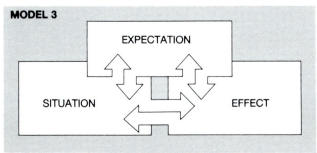

MODEL 3

Determining the relevant importance of each factor to an individual's pattern of drug use should provide a pointer towards the logical treatment response.

Effect – It is clearly not possible to become dependent upon an experience which does not change the feelings or mood of the user. These effects of drugs were raised in Chapter 2 where the problems that can be caused by mood altering substances were discussed.

Situation – In Chapter 3 we examined the circumstances in which people might turn to drugs. For instance, almost one third of all US troops in Vietnam were believed to be heavily addicted to heroin. Despite alarming predictions about what would happen to these users, research conducted by Lee Robins (1974) found that only seven per cent became readdicted after they returned home. One of the surprising findings was that many of those who continued use did so in a recreational way with a large measure of control over the habit. Clearly the change in situation for these users was very significant.

Expectation – The influence of expectations on people's experiences of drugs was examined in Chapter 2. Apart from the effects of believing in the power of specific substances, expectation also involves personal value systems and how people see themselves. Any intervention or treatment model geared towards achieving abstinence is likely to fail if it does not offer alternative strategies which help users to readjust their level of self-belief and esteem.

An assessment model of the type outlined above can be useful in developing a rational problem-solving approach to treatment.

ACTIVITY 6.5
KEY ASSESSMENT QUESTIONS

You should spend 20 minutes on this activity.

John is 25. Eight years ago he was sent to Borstal on a charge of grievous bodily harm after stabbing a friend during a pub brawl. On release he sought out the two prosecution witnesses at his trial and attacked them. One young man was hospitalized with severe facial injuries. John received a further custodial sentence. Over the years he continued to commit crimes of violence and occasionally threatened those working with him. He is close to his family although on two occasions he has attacked his father. However, during the past nine months his behaviour appears to have changed a great deal. He seems more amenable and has stayed out of trouble. Recently he has been charged with possession of cannabis. Normally this would only result in a fine in court but with his previous record he is concerned that he might be imprisoned again. He admits using cannabis regularly over the past nine months and claims it has a calming effect on him. He says he now feels more in control of his anger and has no intention of stopping his cannabis smoking.

Imagine that you have been working with John as a probation officer (or as any other equally responsible practitioner) since he was first sent to Borstal and that during this time you have maintained a good relationship with him, although he has threatened you with violence in the past.

Bearing in mind the points raised by Thorley in Activity 6.4 and, referring to the three headings on effect, situation and expectation, write down some questions you would want to ask at an assessment interview with John.

Comment

A constructive assessment would probably examine the relative importance of the following factors:

Effect – Did he use more than one type of drug? Are there any particular drugs that would not be used? How do they make the user feel? Has the drug user ever felt like that in any other circumstance? Has there ever been an attempt to stop and how did that feel?

Situation – Are there friends who do not use cannabis or other drugs? Have any of these friends stopped and what happened to them? What are his prospects in employment, relationships, housing etc.? Are the user and/or his friends interested or involved in any other activities?

Expectation – How would the drug user describe himself? How does the user think other people see him? What is felt about the differences between these two pictures? What would be the perfect picture and what would have to be done to achieve this? Where does the user feel he might end up if using cannabis is/isn't stopped?

Of course, this is by no means an exhaustive list of questions and practitioners should develop their own set to suit themselves and the individual circumstances.

6.4   CHOOSING THE RESPONSE

Assessment procedures should help in determining the details of the response that might be offered to the drug user. These tend to fall into two broad categories, non-drug options and treatment-based options.

NON-DRUG OPTIONS

As we saw in the paper by Thorley it is probably not a good idea to start work with drug users by focusing exclusively on their use of drugs. Abstinence has also

been questioned as the inevitable goal of any treatment intervention.

There are situations where beginning with the drug problem may be inappropriate. Examples might include working with pregnant drug users where withdrawal could be dangerous for the foetus, or working in custodial establishments where withdrawal has been involuntary. Moreover, if it is true that the expansion of the drug subculture has led to a more 'normal' average profile, then, logically, future directions for drug treatment services will move slowly away from the social work model and begin to develop initiatives based on leisure and recreation.

However, such an approach leads us back to the dilemma in choosing between abstinence and harm reduction approaches to treatment that we discussed in Chapter 5.

Less contentious, though, is the provision of health care advice to drug users. Increasingly, practitioners are coming to see this as a vital element in their face-to-face work. To some extent this development has been sharpened by concern about the spread of the AIDS virus within the drug using community. Gradually, advice on needle-sharing is beginning to be expanded to include safer sex, dealing with overdoses, nutrition, ante-natal care/advice etc. This is probably a particularly useful initiative. Since many drug users make a number of attempts at abstinence, their contact with a treatment agency can be influential in spreading information to the rest of the drug subculture. Experience has shown, for instance, that the majority of fatal overdoses take place in the company of others. This could mean, therefore, that these overdoses are, at least potentially, avoidable. We suggest that practitioners prepare their own check list covering advice on overdose which they give to users. This might include:

- Get information on the cause/what taken/when
- Check pulse and breathing every 5–10 minutes
- If drowsy, stimulate
- If unconscious, phone for an ambulance
- If not breathing, give mouth to mouth resuscitation
- If no pulse, give heart massage
- If tense and panicking, reassure
- On signs of recovery, treat for shock

(We recommend R.H. Campbell 'Overdose Aid' as a useful resource for information on this subject.)

TREATMENT-BASED OPTIONS

In any intervention four possible options will be available to the practitioner – counselling, therapy, advice-giving and control. Whilst it is useful to separate these options for discussion, in practice the practitioner will probably adopt a more pragmatic approach often using more than one option during a single session.

In a *counselling* session the practitioner would seek to encourage the drug user to discuss the main problems and aim at clarifying possible options for their solution. Occasionally the counsellor will summarize the information to help the drug user to put them into some sort of order.

Advice-giving on the other hand, involves giving users information which they did not have before. In some ways, therefore, counselling and advice-giving are opposites. However, a practitioner can, where necessary, change from one form of help to the other, provided the intention is signalled to, and accepted by, the client.

Therapy involves a more concentrated attempt to encourage a client to experience or re-experience particular feelings in a safe environment. Longer lasting changes in personality and lifestyles are also often concerns of therapy. A therapist might change from counselling to therapy and back again in a session but should always signal this intention and gain the user's permission.

Control can also be an important part of the drug worker's practice. Control may involve negotiating and clarifying what behaviour is and is not acceptable in the therapeutic relationship, how any disputes can be managed, and the ultimate aims of the intervention. Control may involve taking decisions about certain actions which are of more benefit to other clients, or even the reputation and continued credibility of the organization, than they are for the good of an individual user. Again such negotiating procedures may be adopted at any time but it should be clear to the user what is happening and why.

6.5   PRACTICAL CONSIDERATIONS

TREATMENT INTERVENTIONS

In the preceding discussion we have looked at suggestions for good practice with drug users. Before we go on to examine how these might be used in treatment strategies, we will look at some impressions of interventions by two drug users.

ACTIVITY 6.6
USERS' VIEWS ON INTERVENTIONS
(Activity 7 on audio)
Spend about 30 minutes on this activity.

Carl, a married man in his early twenties, referred himself to a helping agency after being arrested for theft. Nick is also in his early twenties and referred himself to the same agency following a suggestion from his probation officer.

When Carl and Nick were interviewed they were asked about current and previous efforts to reduce their drug use. Listen to the audio cassette and make brief notes on what you think each found helpful or unhelpful in their efforts to reduce their drug use. Give reasons for your choices.

Comment

You may have identified specific things for each of these men and you will probably have recognized that they have in common a positive self-image, seeing themselves as 'normal lads' who have done 'silly things'.

They have rejected intervention approaches that lower their self-esteem and seem to value approaches which broaden their options and give them more choices. One option, which may be the best 'choice' from their points of view, is probably a reduced sentence gained by being on a voluntary drugs programme. If this is so then it would provide the leading treatment edge, which would open up the opportunity to review and work on both the primary and secondary problems.

In the diagram opposite we have tried to identify the complex relationships between assessment concerns, treatment objectives, the user's expectations and the practitioner's skills which go into making up an intervention process.

Thorley says that history taking will involve concentrating on the problems the user perceives he/she has, and avoids talking about drug taking as the central issue. It's important to explore motivation for attending the session and for the users to work through why they think attendance might help.

In learning about a drug taking career it is important to remember to identify effect, situation and expectation. You might like to look back at your responses to Activity 6.5 to remind yourself of key assessment questions to be used when taking a history.

In assessing the importance of effect, situation and expectation you can encourage the user to focus on patterns of use by having them complete exercises similar to Activities 6.1 and 6.3. Listing advantages and disadvantages of use, and drawing a personal map showing influences on use will help you both to identify when significant dress rehearsals and significant high-risk situations occured. This baseline information should be useful when setting goals aimed at modifying consumption.

A detailed assessment of this sort could also provide a view of the user's self-esteem. If this is low some social skills or assertiveness training might be built into the programme.

Treatment is based on assessment information which can be used to work out realistic treatment goals. Before goal setting can occur, however, it is necessary to check out the degree and accuracy of information that the user holds. Further information may need to be given (about the effects of withdrawal, for example) before realistic goals can be agreed.

Goals may be spoken or written and may take the form of a priority list of problems to tackle, a contract, or a series of diary entries. It is best if they can be written down so that there is a record of shared commitment

TREATMENT SKILLS

ESTABLISHING THE RELATIONSHIP

- Acceptance of the drug user as a person with problems is crucial
- Empathic and understanding practitioners are more likely to form successful relationships with drug users
- Drug users should be accepted in a warm and friendly way and practitioners should be able to give reassurance and praise. Consider talking about your own experiences
- Think about the setting in which the intervention (treatment) takes place. Can the user feel relaxed?

ASSESSMENT STRATEGIES

- What has been the 'career' of drug use over the years?
- What are the present patterns of use? What is a typical day?
- What effects does the user expect from the drug use?
- In what situations or settings are the drugs used?
- Direct or demanding questions usually do not work. A slower, more systematic, approach may be more effective
- A 'Drug Use Diary' may be an effective way of revealing patterns of drug use to the user
- A 'balance sheet' could show the pros and cons of particular drug use choices
- The interview situation could involve giving information on hazardous drugs and methods of use. Honest, accurate information about the legal aspects of drug use could be helpful. Information about coping with an overdose could save lives. Consider giving out literature/leaflets etc.

NON-DRUG PROBLEMS

- Drug taking may not be the most important feature of the client's life
- Unhappy relationships might be both the cause and effect of drug use
- Dealing with housing problems, employment issues, poverty, etc., may be important in assisting the user to deal successfully with drug dependency

SETTING GOALS

- Set realistic goals together with the drug user
- Clarify the *order* (sequence) in which the goals or subgoals are to be achieved and ensure that the *timescale* is realistic
- Failure should be regarded as a 'dress rehearsal' in which the client learns from experience in preparation for the next attempt

RELAPSE PREVENTION

- Help the drug user anticipate 'high risk situations' and learn strategies for avoiding these
- Teach coping skills to counteract negative emotional states such as anger, anxiety or boredom, which can all lead to relapse
- Encourage the development of interpersonal skills by the use of assertiveness training, relaxation techniques, gradual exposure to anxiety producing situations, etc.

POSSIBLE STUMBLING BLOCKS

- Fear of effects of withdrawal can lead to continued drug use. Encourage realistic views about withdrawal symptoms
- Avoid counselling (or other treatment interventions) when someone is intoxicated. Include this as a condition in the treatment 'contract'
- Avoid using drug-related jargon. Mistakes may alienate you from the client

REHABILITATION

- A good principle is that everyone has the capacity to choose not to use drugs, to change and to grow
- Personal growth and change can be slow processes and only become apparent over long periods of time
- Work towards avoidance of: intoxication, regular excessive consumption, dependency
- Plan systematic reduction of use, including drug-free times, etc.
- Find safe psychological props
- Help the drug user 'deal with loss' – giving up pleasurable habits is never easy!

statements that show a map of progress over time. A problem with writing down commitment statements, however, is that they look good on paper, but may not reflect real life behaviour. A popular joke is the one about the man in the pub who asks for a pint for himself and an orange juice for the diary.

The helper should be alert to this practice and maintain a certain degree of scepticism about sudden conversion reports. Other signs such as obvious intoxication or further incidents of problem use will be guides to how effective treatment goals are in influencing behaviour.

ACTIVITY 6.7
'RECOGNITION AND TREATMENT OF ALCOHOL-RELATED DISORDERS'

This is an optional activity which should take about 20 minutes to complete.

Ritson in his paper, 'Recognition and treatment of alcohol-related disorders', in the Reader, recognizes the difficulties involved in changing drug (alcohol) taking behaviour and advocates the drawing up of a balance sheet to motivate changes in consumption. He recommends the use of a drinking diary to both record progress and identify high-risk times. You may now like to read this article.

Comment

Modification of consumption is likely to involve breaking the drug-taking habit by finding safer 'props' than drugs to give comfort in everyday life. For Nick, on the audio cassette in Activity 6.6, the safer props were new activities to fill his day. One in particular, the theatre, became very important to him.

Treatment plans should be directed at modifying or stopping use but it is unlikely that this will be a smooth path. Users therefore need to have a lifeline in an emergency – maybe a phone number that they can use when in a high-risk situation. Whilst high-risk situations should be avoided, it is unrealistic to expect people to suddenly change their lifestyles – and not all high-risk situations can be predicted.

Lapses, mistakes and comforts are all part of everyday life and the user should be encouraged to see them as that, not as a failure of the whole treatment programme.

Relapse prevention

Relapse prevention is an approach to treatment based upon psychological principles of social learning theory. It was developed during the late 1970s and early 1980s, and its goal is to help people who wish to stop using drugs learn how to anticipate and cope with the problem of relapse. It is, therefore, one type of treatment intervention that is concerned with the problem of 'staying off'. Relapse prevention is a self-control programme that combines behavioural skills training, forms of psychological therapy designed to change attitudes, and changes in social patterns of living. The two most important concepts in relapse prevention interventions are 'high-risk situations', and 'coping responses'.

When people succeed in coming off drugs they need to find some way of maintaining their drug-free state. Sooner or later they will run into situations which put them at risk of using again. When this happens their chances of being able to remain drug-free will depend to a large extent upon their ability to cope with the particular situation. Relapse prevention treatments are designed to help users identify the more likely high-risk situations that they may face, and to help them strengthen existing skills, or teach them new skills, for coping with these situations.

Negative emotional states, such as anger, anxiety, depression or (very commonly with adolescents) boredom, are amongst the more frequently noted problems. Another area of difficulty involves social interactions with other people. Situations involving conflict within a social relationship (notably marriage, the family, or employer–employee relations) are often mentioned as difficult high-risk situations. A considerable proportion of relapses also occur as a result of social pressure. This may involve active pressure from others (as when the user meets an old drug-using friend who tries to persuade him or her to take drugs again), or it may involve more indirect and subtle forms of pressure (such as simply being with other people who are known to be using drugs, even though no direct pressure is involved).

The identification and analysis of high-risk situations, however, is only a beginning in teaching the individual how to cope with them. The establishment of adequate coping techniques involves a wide range of psychological methods as well as more straightforward restructuring of lifestyles. Many users who are dependent upon drugs may also have difficulty in being

A high risk situation?

appropriately assertive. Where this represents an identified high-risk situation, treatment may involve a course
in assertiveness training. Where there are high levels of
anxiety which are relieved by drug taking, part of the
relapse prevention treatment could involve anxiety-
reducing methods such as relaxation training or gradual
exposure to the anxiety-raising situation. When an identified high-risk situation exists in the environment other
methods may be appropriate. For example, if a person
is likely to be put at risk of relapsing because of sharing
a flat with habitual drug users, the relapse prevention
programme should include improved accommodation
within its targets for change.

Referring on

There may be some treatment or rehabilitation skills that
you cannot offer. Everyone needs to recognize their
limitations and know when and how to refer to other
agencies. This means maintaining a good working
knowledge of local facilities and resources, as suggested in Activities 1.6 and 1.7 in Chapter 1.

THE DIY APPROACH

As we begin to understand more about drug use, the
process whereby people move in and out of drug use
will become a little clearer. You will know from reading
Chapter 3 that the vast majority of those who become
involved in drug use do so on an experimental basis
and even those whose use becomes a regular feature
of their lives rarely suffer the sort of emotional and
physical trauma associated with the stereotypical
'junkie'.

Those who do experience problems with their drug use
will most likely achieve abstinence without recourse to
specialist or even generic agencies. The majority of
people who stop using drugs do so on their own or with
the help of friends and/or relatives. As with former
cigarette smokers the process is a varied one and often
involves a number of attempts.

There is clearly a great deal more which could be done
to encourage this process both by providing help and
encouragement to the friends and relatives of users and
by disseminating accurate non-alarmist advice about
'DIY' withdrawal.

Much of this advice and support will take a similar form
to that which is given face-to-face in treatment situations.
Since it is to be given indirectly it is important that such
advice is clear, straightforward and flexible. The reader
should be able to adapt any such information material
to his/her own particular circumstances (for further information on this see *How to stop,* a short booklet
prepared by staff from the Blenheim Project, a London-
based street agency).

ACTIVITY 6.8
HELPING PETER TO STOP

*This is an optional activity which should take
about 30 minutes.*

Imagine you are working in a busy inner-city area
office. You are approached by Peter, a 21 year
old student. His drug use began in earnest whilst
at college, although during his last years at
school he had taken amphetamine regularly in
order to stay awake for long periods of study.

During his examinations he had stolen some of his father's valium tablets to calm his anxiety. Whilst at college his use of both heroin and amphetamine became more extravagant and a great deal more visible. The college authorities eventually decided to expel him but his case was taken up by the student union who argued successfully for a year's sabbatical. That was nine months ago. His parents have refused to have anything to do with him since his suspension.

He lives in a small bedsit in a run-down area of the city with little realistic hope of improved housing. During the year he has attended the psychiatric in-patient ward for methadone detoxification but left after three days because: 'They all treated me like dirt and said I'd brought it all upon myself anyway'. Since then he has tried once to stop on his own. He started on the Tuesday evening and stayed at home until the Thursday morning when he had to attend the Social Security office to collect his giro. There he met up with some other drug users and quickly agreed to go to a local dealer to 'score' for them and himself. That was three weeks ago and according to Peter: 'I'm bang at it again. Things are worse now than they ever were'. He seems desperate to stop but adamant that he will not return to the psychiatric hospital; the only specialist service in the area.

Referring to the paper by Thorley which you studied in Activity 6.4 write short notes on what advice you would give to Peter on:

(a) timing

(b) assistance

(c) procedure

when helping him to plan a strategy for his next home detoxification attempt.

Comment

The strategy might include at least the following:

Timing – Peter should be helped to plan the timing and situation in which the attempt is made. Going to collect his giro is obviously a high-risk situation. He might be advised to begin withdrawing on a Friday and/or (depending on how he feels) not going himself the following week but giving the letter of authorization to the person who is supporting his withdrawal. The person authorized needs to be trustworthy and not likely to 'score' with the money!

Assistance – He should try to get help from a friend for the whole period of the actual physical withdrawal. This is unlikely to be more than one or two weeks, although he is likely to feel extremely delicate for some weeks and will be susceptible to any number of minor ailments: coughs, colds etc. Support might be available from a friend who also wishes to withdraw at the same time. However, if this has been tried before, serious consideration should be given to a different approach. The amount of support Peter's GP can give should be explored.

Procedure – He should be advised to reduce daily dosage as much as possible before the actual attempt is made. Further advice could be given about keeping warm, occupied, well-fed etc. during the course of the withdrawal.

Reassurance – Many drug users believe the counsels of despair which are fed to them by the media and public opinion. They need to know that others have successfully withdrawn and that help is available to them if things begin to get difficult. Finally, they need to be encouraged that there is no such thing as a last chance. Many people do manage to stop at the first attempt but many more need a number of 'dress rehearsals'. These should not be seen as failures but as opportunities for learning what changes need to be made for the future attempt. Above all, guidelines should contain reassurance that a small slip backwards should not necessarily mean a U-turn all the way back to the beginning.

The final point is of great importance and is only now beginning to be better recognized by practitioners. Marlatt (1982) in Washington investigated a whole range of 'failures' from treatment programmes for compulsive overeaters, alcoholics, cigarette smokers and heroin addicts. In almost every case, the relapse had been preceded by a lapse which, objectively, need not have done very much damage to overall progress.

Furthermore, it appears that lapse/relapse can become cross-transferrable. Thus in Portage, a therapeutic community for drug users in Canada, research showed that reintroduction to drug dependency was often preceded by bouts of heavy drinking (Devlin, 1986).

Marlatt concluded that many agencies, by placing such a high premium on 'success' allowed no more room for discussion of potential stumbles. This meant that as soon as a slip was made, the experience undermined the individual's self-image as an abstainer and left nowhere to go back to a previous (tried and tested) alternative. In encouraging drug users to stop using or at least moderate their use we are asking them to learn or relearn a skill. As with any other skill the beginner is more likely to stand out for his mistakes than his genius.

SOME BASIC STUMBLING BLOCKS

Any form of treatment intervention aimed at achieving permanent change in a pattern of problem drug use will potentially involve a long-term commitment from both the practitioner and the drug user. Most generic practitioners already possess the necessary skills, and will need only to understand and accept that these skills are relevant and that there is nothing mystical about drug use. However, there are some common difficulties which in some ways are peculiar to drugs:

Manipulation – It is often said that drug users are manipulative (although manipulation by the practitioner is rarely questioned). The use of this expression may be a convenient way of avoiding important questions about the practitioner's own attitudes towards drug use and his/her perception of the treatment process as an agent of social control. It normally means that the goals and expectations of the practitioner are in conflict with those of the drug user, that the user has the skills to achieve his/her goals and – crucially – that these goals are usually disapproved of by the practitioner. Clearly, the only way of avoiding this situation is to be open and honest about attitudes and expectations and to explore where this differs from the drug user's own perception of needs and problems. From this foundation an agreement or contract can be made which describes the limits of the relationship, and sets out common ground and a series of agreed goals.

Intoxication – Part of this contract should relate to intoxication during counselling sessions. Whilst most practitioners will not be expecting instant abstinence they would rightly expect the drug users to be sober enough to communicate coherently and be able to understand what is said. The use of most drugs will radically alter mood and perception and this can make

any interaction virtually useless. The alteration in mood may lead the user to make commitments which he/she is unable or unwilling to keep and which can cause guilt and anxiety on 'sobering up'. A practitioner in such circumstances should confine him/herself to either basic first aid or the arrangement of another appointment, whichever appears the most appropriate.

Talking about drugs – Whilst it may be extremely interesting and informative to spend time discussing drugs and their effects, this is rarely a useful exercise for the dependent drug user and can reinforce the 'junkie image' of a social outlaw in a secret society. The therapeutic interview is neither the time nor the place to extend the practitioner's knowledge base on drugs.

Denial – Drug users will often deny their usage or that they have used on a particular occasion. This is part of a behaviour pattern which has often developed over a considerable period of time. There are often good reasons, rooted in societal disapproval and the illegality of some drugs, which can make such denial almost a reflex. And it can reflect the drug user's difficulty in 'opening up to' parts of him/herself which are particularly painful and resistant to change. Entering into a 'yes you are – no I'm not' argument is time consuming, frustrating and inevitably unproductive. The practitioner in these circumstances should simply state his/her belief, acknowledge that this is a difficult area for the user at this stage and move on to look at some of the problems which might lie behind the denial.

DEALING WITH DEFEAT

It is rather easy to sit back and discuss concepts of lapse and relapse and 'dress rehearsals'. The experience takes on a different meaning for both the practitioner/friend/relative and for the drug user when it actually happens.

Workers in drug agencies have had to come to terms with the difficulties of seeing the collapse of what appear to be foolproof and mutually acceptable strategies. They have had to develop sensitive and, hopefully, productive ways of dealing with the negative feelings both of the practitioner and the client in this situation. Specialist agencies are at something of an advantage in this situation, since they are able to offer reassurance to the drug user by pointing to or describing other similar situations which have had a happy outcome. Friends and relatives and workers in some generic agencies are less likely to have such experiences and an invitation to despair may appear more attractive.

It is vital in these circumstances to explore events in detail with the drug user and try to spot where things went wrong. An early repeat attempt can often pre-empt a return to the original situation but adjustment should always be made for the problems identified the previous time. More of the same is rarely helpful. Short-term, relatively modest interim goals can help to give a feeling of momentum and provide a series of markers which the individual can cling to in the case of further stumbles.

Finally, it is of course important for the helper — whether paid or unpaid, specialist or generic — to recognize the need for support and advice for him/herself. This is particularly so when things appear to have gone badly wrong. It can be all too easy to become disillusioned not only with the drug user but with oneself. Recognize that you need support to help you work through ideas and feelings and to help you get a balanced perspective on responsibility. It will be helpful if you are able to share ideas, decisions, defeats and successes with your colleagues.

REFERENCES

Blenheim Project, *How to stop*

Campbell, R. H. 'Overdose Aid', The Lifeline Project

Devlin, C. (1978) in an unpublished paper presented at a workshop at the 'Third World Conference on Therapeutic Communities' in Rome in 1978

Marlatt, A. (1982) Unpublished review

Robins, L. N. (1974) 'Drug use by US army enlisted men in Vietnam: a follow-up on their return home', *American Journal of Epidemiology* 99 (4)

Russell, M. A. H. (1976) 'What is Dependency?' in Edwards, G. (1976) *Drugs and Drug Dependency*, Lexicon Books

7 SUMMARY AND LOOKING FORWARD

PART I

7.1 INTRODUCTION

We introduced the course with a reading which discussed some of the more dramatic attitudes ('moral panics') that people sometimes have about the use, or rather misuse, of certain drugs. We also noted that there are legal drugs which are readily available and widely used by very many people. Some of these drugs are known to be harmful (say, tobacco) and some (such as alcohol) are associated with accidents and ill health far in excess of any equivalent injury caused by some of the illicit drugs. This concern about certain drugs and toleration or even promotion of others sets the scene for our understanding of the permanent presence of drug use in all societies.

In this course we are concerned about drugs which act on the brain to produce changes in mood or psychological functioning, and clearly these drugs have the capacity both to give pleasure and to cause suffering. Perhaps it is not surprising, therefore, that human beings have rather ambiguous feelings and a somewhat 'love–hate' relationship with these mood changing drugs. So, although a great deal of human ingenuity and time continues to be spent in preparing and distributing drugs, societies also spend a lot of energy trying to reduce and even eliminate the same drugs! In the discussions in Chapter 3 on the use and misuse of drugs and in Chapter 4 on the control of drugs we noted the changing patterns of use. Sometimes these changes only show over a period of time, as communities and their fashions change. Sometimes the change is rapid, for example when large cheap quantities of a drug become available on the market. What does not seem to change, however, is the persistent use of drugs by people of all societies.

7.2 HOW IS DRUG USE AND MISUSE TO BE UNDERSTOOD?

Possible factors leading to drug use are summarized in the diagram overleaf. These factors were discussed in Chapters 2 and 3.

But whatever motivates an individual to use drugs, ambiguities remain. On the one hand, using drugs can be very pleasant, and on the other hand, their use or misuse can lead to many problems, such as with the law. Similar ambiguities exist at the societal level. In Chapters 1 and 4, for example, we noted that the production of illicit drugs can sometimes make a significant contribution to a country's economy. At the same time the growth of powerful criminal syndicates who control the illicit drugs industry can corrupt whole layers of society which become open to bribery and illegal activities.

Bearing this in mind it may be fruitful to view the continuing presence of illicit drugs in society, despite campaigns for their eradication, as the outcome of permanent tensions at the personal and societal levels. The continued presence and use of drugs is clouded in ambiguities which both contribute to, and detract from, personal needs and national economic concerns.

At the personal level, these tensions, as we saw in Chapters 2 and 3, are influenced by the set and settings in which the drugs are used. The user must balance the positive pleasures of drug use against the hassle of getting them, the attitudes of others, the threat of legal sanctions, and the effects of a lifestyle which may leave little time or inclination for other interests, and so on.

MISUSE OF DRUGS; CAUSAL FACTORS

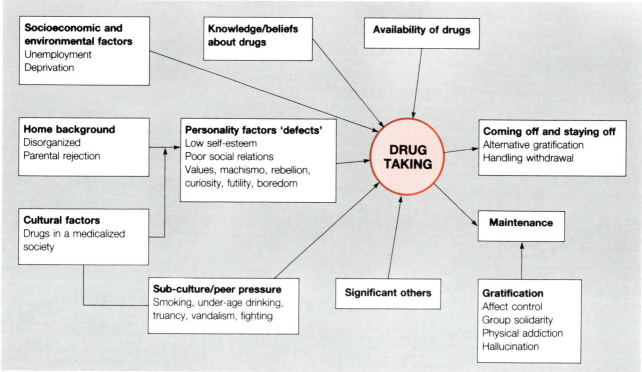

At the societal level the tensions seem to arise as a conflict between political (and moral) and economic considerations. The drugs economy, we noted in several places, provides a source of income to the farmer, the manufacturer and the retailer. At the same time, the manufacture and circulation of drugs provides revenue for governments (taxes on legal drugs) and foreign exchange for hard-pressed debtor Third World economies. It also contributes to the black economy which, especially under conditions of economic depression, may sustain a considerable number of people. Under these conditions, the farmer, as we saw in Chapter 4, faces difficult moral and economic choices when under pressure from the government to stop drug cultivation.

7.3   ATTITUDES AND INFLUENCES ON DRUG USE

From early experimentation to dependency the business of attaining and using drugs, it was suggested in Chapter 3, is an active process. The 'drug user career' was put forward as a useful model for interpreting the choices and changes that take place in the life of a user. From this point of view the user can be seen as facing choices at critical 'transition' points in his or her career. Changes in personal relations – such as conflicts with parents, rejection by loved ones, being arrested for 'possession', changes in the supply and price of the preferred drug – influence the balance between the positive and negative implications of drug use. This, in turn, may lead the user further into dependency or open up possibilities of seeking help.

At the societal level changes in the availability and attractiveness of drugs due to factors such as new sources of supply, the arrival of new drugs, cheaper production methods, changing attitudes in different countries, changing ability to control the manufacture or cultivation of drugs, more effective transport systems for moving drugs from production site to the market, all influence social attitudes and governmental choices. From this point of view social attitudes, such as those presented in sudden and erratic press campaigns ('moral panics'), may be interpreted as a response to a changing balance in the tension between a drug's attraction and its harmful effects. The presence of myths, such as those which imply that drug users are inactive and mostly in their youth, that withdrawal is an extreme experience involving pain and sickness, and that once certain drugs are taken they can't be stopped, further influences the meaning a drug acquires at the social level.

7.4   THE SEARCH FOR A RATIONAL APPROACH TO INTERVENTION

As the balance between the advantages and disadvantages of drug use at the personal and societal levels changes, pressure may grow to increase the level of intervention in order to maintain some kind of rational control over drug use. In this sense intervention can be viewed as a more systematic attempt to regulate the balance between the contradictory advantages and disadvantages of human drug use. At the personal level the various approaches to treatment aim at helping the individual reduce or stop drug use by acquiring the necessary skills to operate more effective self-constraint or by some other technique which makes drug use less attractive. At the societal level intervention aims to reduce the availability of drugs through a range of measures, from eradication of drug bearing crops, more stringent customs controls, more effective policing and harsher penalties (making it less attractive to manufacture and distribute drugs). And there is a third level of intervention, which spans the personal and societal levels. This is concerned with assisting the individual at the social level by developing preventative measures and more effective health promotion programmes.

PART II

Problem drug use does not occur in a vacuum. It is influenced by the conditions and events of everyday living. So, if interventions aimed at reducing use are to be successful, attention must be directed at societal as well as individual strategies.

7.5   PRIMARY AND SECONDARY PREVENTION

'Preventing drug problems' by Les Kay in the Course Reader notes the need for both primary and secondary prevention of drug problems. Primary prevention means stopping people from beginning to use drugs – usually by mass education campaigns – whilst secondary prevention means reducing harm associated with drug use. The main discussion in the course has been concerned with secondary prevention. Kay discusses the need for both approaches while observing that, to date, most resources have been directed at primary prevention. This strategy seems to have been generally ineffective.

ACTIVITY 7.1
A WIDER COMMUNITY RESPONSE TO DRUG USE

Spend one hour on this activity.

You should now read the paper 'Preventing drug problems' by Les Kay. As you do so make notes on:

(a) the Drug Advisory Council's criteria for intervention

(b) why Kay believes that the primary prevention strategies used have not worked

(c) the 'social action' options advocated by Kay

(d) the social policy implications of these 'social actions'.

Comment

(a) The Drug Advisory Council's criteria for prevention are:

● reducing the risk of an individual engaging in drug misuse (primary prevention)

● reducing the harm associated with drug misuse (secondary prevention).

(b) In Kay's view primary prevention strategies have not worked because the gap between knowledge and behaviour has not been addressed – just knowing about drugs does not affect drug related behaviour. Other writers (Howe, Course Reader; Davies, 1986) also make this point.

Kay offers an explanation of why primary prevention has has had little effect. He suggests that prevention and education, although they are thought to, do not go hand in hand. Personal and social education (PSE) encourages individual autonomy/empowerment, whereas primary prevention is based on the assumption that (if the approach is right) young people will respond collectively.

(c) 'Social action' options suggested are: housing and unemployment initiatives, and action on welfare rights. These initiatives will need social policy action at local and national levels.

(d) A number of social policy implications are apparent. The first of these concerns the need for interagency/government-department collaboration. Clear policy decisions based on available information and expertise are important. The harm reduction approach should be explored for the potential contribution that it can make. Health promotion strategies, directed at influencing lifestyle choices and social changes may also be employed. These include:

● public education on problems of legal and illegal drug use. In addition to providing accurate information about drugs and drug use this would serve to demystify use of illegal drugs and so allow people to feel more able to respond

● local authority policy on drug advertisements, such as, withholding permission for poster sites

● an increase in training resources for workers in the field. Primary preventative measures currently employed (mass advertising) lead to a greater demand on and for services

● the sharing of helping skills and greater use of local voluntary personnel. This would help in making services more 'user friendly'

● greater use of key local and national opinion leaders and the mass media to sensitise the community to success stories/new initiatives. This type of critical consciousness raising can help to change the general climate in which drugs are viewed

● workplace policies and intervention services aimed at preventing/assisting in the reduction of problem drug use. Many large companies now have smoking and drinking policies.

There are several levels of intervention concerned with preventing drug problems. These might be summarized in the following way:

Levels of interventions

Level	Action
Individual	Understand your own drug use
Work with clients	Use your new understanding to develop your counselling skills and improve sensitivity in suggesting strategies for your clients
Work with drug-related projects	Better co-ordination between helping agencies
Community level	Drug services should be seen in the context of other activities that might improve the community and provide alternatives for vulnerable people to join in with – improved housing; employment opportunities will lessen the need for people to resort to the use of drugs
Statutory service provision, Health Authority level, Social Services etc.	Each Authority should have a well worked out policy about drug users
Specialist services, regional policy and national (Government) policy	Clearly worked out national and regional policies based on Advisory Committee on Misuse of Drugs recommendations (for example, North West Regional Health Authority Drugs Misuse Policy)

7.6 HEALTH PROMOTION

Tones (1986) notes that non-drug-specific health promotion strategies may have greater implications for prevention than drug-specific strategies. This is because they recognize and seek to influence the wide range of factors affecting drug use. He says: 'Health promotion incorporates education, but also includes other preventive strategies such as social engineering. It is well recognised that education is but one com-

ponent in a series of measures designed to combat drug misuse. These include various regulatory tactics involving police and customs as well as the provision of counselling and treatment services. Less obvious factors, such as whether or not doctors favour the prescription of methadone replacement therapy as opposed to abrupt withdrawal, may also have an impact on the nature and level of abuse. It is, however, the non-drug-specific health promotion strategies which may have greater implications for prevention. In so far as hard drug abuse is associated with general deprivation or particular social ills, such as unemployment, any health promotion measures which are found to be effective in remedying social and structural concomitants of disease will also presumably contribute to the prevention of drug related problems'.

Tones also recognizes the need for personal and social education to enable people to make lifestyle choices, and feel comfortable about the decisions they make. Lifeskills (including social skills) training helps develop self-image and self-esteem. You will recall PSE as a component of many of the programmes offered by intervention agencies (described in Chapter 5).

Another important component of PSE, social education, is described by Tones. This 'complements the individualistic orientation of lifeskills teaching with a collectivist approach. Its main goal is that of critical consciousness raising (political education) – it draws attention to the society in which we live and seeks to generate concern about, for instance, social injustice'.

The promotion of social change is also discussed by Barbara Howe, in a paper in the Course Reader. In it she discusses this as one of the features of a drug education campaign. In talking about what a campaign might realistically do she identifies potential to:

● increase accurate factual awareness

● reduce prejudice and stereotyping

● promote social change by altering the social climate.

This paper also contains an account of the Tyne Tees Alcohol Education Campaign. This is a particularly valuable account in that weaknesses as well as strengths are described. Of particular note in the account is the description of the shift in the campaign approach from an abstinence approach to a harm reduction one – advocating a policy of sensible drinking. Evaluation of the campaign concluded that: 'What it has done is to provide a context in which people now seem willing to talk and think about alcohol use in new and constructive ways'.

One problem, identified in the paper, is the unrealistic expectations often attached to drug campaigns. There are also often unrealistic, or untested, claims of success in terms of reported behaviour change. These should be interpreted with caution: 'any evaluation can only be discussed with respect to the stated aims of the communications to be evaluated. Thus, if the aims are to change verbal behaviour or stated attitudes, then the proper stuff of the evaluation is in fact verbal statements, attitudes, and so on – if changes in verbal behaviour constitute the main aims and goals of a campaign, then no generalisation beyond those kinds of data is permissible. Furthermore, it would be helpful to the public at large to know that the aim of such a drug education campaign was to change the verbal answers that people would give – rather than to reduce drug abuse in some way' (Davies, 1986).

Davies goes on to urge that drug campaigns be aimed at modifying use and that evaluation, designed to assess changes in use, must be an integral component of any campaign.

7.7 TACKLING THE PROBLEM: CO-ORDINATED PLANNING

A developing theme of this chapter has been the imbalance between primary and secondary prevention approaches. Kay, Howe and Davies have discussed the resources spent on, and the influence of, mass education drug campaigns. Earlier in this chapter it was argued that more resources should be provided for secondary prevention, and, in particular, for education and training for drug workers. Resources should also be invested in local housing, employment, welfare services and drug helping agencies if the problem of increasing drug use in the UK is to be tackled effectively.

The need for co-ordinated planning and provision of health, health education and social welfare services has been identified. This type of activity is now occurring under the general umbrella of health promotion. Regional Health Promotion Plans have been developed as a response to the need to meet UK (WHO 1986) lifestyle targets. These targets have been developed for all member countries of the WHO European Region. Target 17 is concerned with drug misuse and calls for a significant decrease in health damaging behaviour. The targets are based on the philosophy that people can and should take responsibility for their own health and welfare. This is not rooted in the 'victim blaming' approach (people use drugs because they are too weak willed to resist them), but is based on a social casualty explanation. Health is seen as a personal and community resource, which is necessary to achieve social actions. Ashton et al. (1986) describe this approach as going 'beyond the historical focus on biological understanding and recognizing the importance of those social aspects of health problems that are related to lifestyle'. This approach is apparent in Regional Health Promotion Plans developed for both Merseyside and the North West. The common objectives are:

- promotion of healthy lifestyles
- prevention of preventable conditions
- rehabilitation.

The problem of drug misuse is described in the North West Health Authority's 10 year regional plan, where a collaborative strategy for tackling the problem is outlined. This is shown in the figure below.

TACKLING THE PROBLEMS OF DRUG MISUSE

IT is estimated that there are between 2,500 and 5,000 drug misusers throughout the region, with particular problems in all Greater Manchester Districts, Blackburn, Burnley and the Skelmersdale area of West Lancashire. We think the problem may get worse before it gets better. So it is a high priority for the NHS. Here are some of the improvements in services we wish to see over the strategy period:

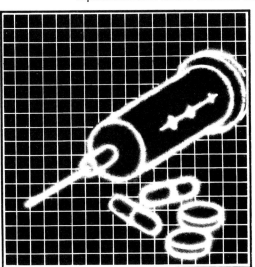

(i) the Prestwich Hospital-based **Regional Drug Dependence Unit** to move to a community setting with:

- an **in-patient unit** of up to 20 beds;
- a small in-patient **assessment unit** separate from the main unit;
- an **out-patient clinic** separate from the in-patient unit;
- **satellite clinics** in all Districts;
- increased **urine screening** facilities;
- training, education and preventive activities;
- research projects.

(ii) **community drug problem teams** (already established in four Districts) to be functioning in every District within the next two years;

(iii) an increasing involvement of *"Lifeline Project"* workers in the rehabilitation of patients with drug-related illnesses;

(iv) **health education** initiatives including:

- primary prevention in reducing the numbers becoming drug misusers;
- secondary prevention or 'damage reduction' in minimising risks to misusers;
- educational programmes for schools;
- a possible pilot project in Salford District during the early part of the period to serve as a model for the rest of the region.

The type of approach shown in this figure has been advocated for the UK since the early 70s by the Advisory Council on the Misuse of Drugs. In the 'Treatment and Rehabilitation Report' (1982) it is identified that the drugs problem is not so much a health service problem, a social work or probation problem, but a multicausal problem.

The North West Community Drugs Teams (described by Strang, one of the initiators, in the Reader paper you read for Chapter 5) are based on this philosophy. The Co-ordinator of the North West Regional Drug Training Unit, Les Kay, gave his interpretation of the approach during an interview with a member of the Course Team:

'In the past we assumed that, because drug use was seen as a medical problem − it was a disease called drug addiction − obviously the response was a medical response. We're now seeing that the range of problems is very wide, and we're talking about things like education and housing and finance and employment and personal relationships, then the range of resources available to respond to the problem needs to be equally wide. And, in fact, we're now trying to mobilize what I suppose you could describe as the whole human service network into a potential response to the whole range of drug problems. So within our area we have what we call community drugs teams, and they're small teams, locally based, district funded − usually from a variety of sources, and the team aims to pull together the community; and the resources available within the community. Whether those are health service resources, social service resources, the probation service, the youth service, local voluntary groups, self-help groups, parents groups, and so on. To pull together all of those different agencies and allow them to work efficiently together, so that anybody who comes into contact with any of those agencies who has a drug problem, can, through this networking, gain access to the resources of all the agencies. And it seems to us that's the key issue, at the moment'.

We have singled out one particular approach to illustrate the range of interventions that may arise when a more comprehensive view of drug prevention is adopted. There are, of course, many other approaches to drug prevention and you were introduced to these in the discussion in Chapter 5. Treatment services, however, have still not been properly evaluated and at this time it is not possible to be confident in promoting one approach over another. Strang and Stimson is the Reader, for example, say that no single approach is adequate. They suggest that a more fruitful approach to treatment is to have access to a range of responses. In Chapter 5 we suggested that all treatment approaches are moving towards harm reduction strategies of intervention and what is needed is a co-ordinated social policy on drug prevention. You might like to bear these points in mind as you complete the final activity.

ACTIVITY 7.2
WRITE AN ARTICLE FOR A NEWSPAPER ON DRUG MISUSE PREVENTION

Spend 30 minutes on this activity.

Look at the newspaper cuttings that you collected at the beginning of your studies of the course. Examine these and the one reproduced opposite, noting stereotyping, presentation of myths as if they were facts, trivializing of relevant information, distortions and anything else which reveals attitudes towards drug taking and drug misuse prevention.

Write an article for a newspaper which would explain why the media should adopt a more positive approach in support of a drug misuse prevention program. Discuss what measures the newspapers might take in order to make a positive contribution to such a program.

Comment

A large range of issues can be raised in this activity and those used will depend upon the particular approach that you adopt. In our discussions we were particularly struck by the way that a serious research issue was trivialized in the cutting shown. It seems that writing about alcohol is no easy task. Of particular interest is the way in which humour is used to obscure the issues and encourage complacency. We wondered whether such similar complaceny might be shown towards illicit drugs?

CHEERS! TV PUB PROBE GRANT

DIRTY DEN'S drinking habits are about to come under scrutiny from a team of lecturers at Leicester University.

For researchers there are raising their glasses to the cheering news that they have been awarded over £20,000 in grants to study the boozy sessions down at East Enders' Queen Vic and other popular soap opera pubs.

The team at the University's Centre for Mass Communication will be studying the portrayal of alcohol on television, how often it is shown, and whether the viewing public are influenced by watching their telly favourites making merry.

Anders Hansen, one of the lecturers involved in the project, carried out a similar study two years ago, thought then to be the first of its kind in the country.

"One of the things that came out of that original study," said Mr Hanson, "was the fact that most alcohol drunk on TV, apart from in commercials, took place in soap operas.

"It is therefore our intention to analyse the most popular soaps and how much alcohol is consumed and whether it's really necessary."

The Alcohol Education and Research Council awarded the University around £16,000 to carry out their studies, and a further £4,500 has been awarded from The Brewers' Society for a similar research study into the Portrayal of Alcohol on Prime Time Television.

"Most other studies have concentrated on the portrayal of alcohol in advertisements," said Mr Hansen, "so we think it is important to take into account those other areas of television in which alcohol is featured a lot.

"The original study brought a lot of feedback," he added, "from TV companies, and from the anti-social lobby who say there is far too much alcohol portrayed on TV. This was disputed by the pro-alcohol movement which claims there is no scientific evidence linking the portrayal of alcohol on TV and the drinking habits of the viewing public.

"It is certainly an area full of controversy and conflicting evidence and therefore needs further studies into it," said Mr Hansen.

REFERENCES

Ashton, J., Seymour, H., Ingleden, D., Ireland, R., Hopley, E., Parry, A., Ryan, M. and Holborne, A. (1986) 'Promoting the New Public Health in Mersey', *Health Education Journal* Vol. 45 No. 3 pp. 174–179

Davies, J. B. (1986) 'Unresolved problems with mass media drug education campaigns: three cautionary tales', *Health Education: Research* Vol. 1. No. 1, 1986, pp. 69–74

Tones, K. (1986) 'Preventing Drug Misuse: the case for breadth, balance and coherence'. *Health Education Journal,* Vol. 45, No. 4 pp. 224–230

North Western Regional Health Authority: The Health of our Region – a 10 year plan. NWHA 10 year plan

ACKNOWLEDGEMENTS

Grateful acknowledgement is made to the following sources for permission to use material in this course:

Text

Cheers! TV Pub Probe Grant: Leicester Trader, May 6 1987.

Figures

Figure p. 25: based on a diagram from the Health Education Authority, London;
Figure p. 86: Tones, K. 'Preventing drug misuse and the care for breadth, balance and coherence', *Health Education Journal,* vol. 45 no. 4, 1986;
Figure p. 91: North Western Regional Health Authority.

Tables

Table p. 25: Ritson, B. 'Recognition and treatment of alcohol-related disorders', *The Practitioner,* May 1986; *Table p. 29:* Plant, M. *Drugs in Perspective,* 1981, Hodder and Stoughton.

Photographs

Photo p. 9: BBC Hulton Picture Library/Bettmann Archive; *Photos pp. 17 and 32:* David Hoffman; *Photo p. 52:* Kentish Gazette.

Cartoons

Cartoon p. 22: Trouble With Tranquillisers, Release Publications.